wild escapes

For Jacbob, S.L.

To Mac, and my dad, A.M.

wild escapes

Incredible Places to Unwind and Explore

Siân Anna Lewis

Photographs by Annapurna Mellor

 **National Trust**

Published by National Trust Books
An imprint of HarperCollins Publishers
1 London Bridge Street
London
SE1 9GF
www.harpercollins.co.uk

HarperCollins Publishers
Macken House
39/40 Mayor Street Upper
Dublin 1
D01 C9W8
Ireland

First published in 2023

ISBN 978-0-00-855848-2

10 9 8 7 6 5 4 3 2 1

A catalogue record for this book is available from the British Library.

Printed and bound in the UAE by Oriental Press.

If you would like to comment on any aspect of this book, please contact us at
the above address or national.trust@harpercollins.co.uk

National Trust publications are available at National Trust shops or online at
Nationaltrustbooks.co.uk

This book is produced from independently certified FSC ™
paper to ensure responsible forest management.

For more information visit: harpercollins.co.uk/green

Thanks to the wonderful teams at both the National
Trust and HarperCollins, and especially to Emily and
Annapurna for making recce trips to cottages across
the country so much fun.

Contents

Introduction

Within the pages of this book, wonderful escapes await. These wild places to stay in Britain are all unique, from a big yellow school bus and a beached fishing boat to a lighthouse and a floating cabin. But they also have something in common: the magic of hiding away in nature and spending time outdoors, far from computer screens and city limits.

Slow travel, solitude and switching off – however you think of it, reconnecting with nature is good for us. With 82 per cent of people in the UK now living in urban areas, perhaps it's not surprising that there has been renewed focus on the importance of spending time in nature – something which has been proven to benefit both our physical and mental wellbeing. We are awakening to the wonders of exploring closer to home and appreciating the wild places on our doorsteps, and beyond.

> **With 82 per cent of people in the UK now living in urban areas, perhaps it's not surprising that there has been renewed focus on the importance of spending time in nature**

As this book is designed to get you closer to the natural world, it's divided up in an elemental way. Pick the landscape you're longing to escape to, then turn to that section of the book. You'll find ancient trees in Woodland, nodding fields of wildflowers in Meadows and snow-capped hills and tales of derring-do in Moors, Hills & Fells, while Coast and On the Water are there waiting for wild swimmers and sea lovers to dive into.

Each chapter includes a choice of incredible places to stay, from affordable campsites to dreamy, blow-the-budget escapes for those extra special occasions.

As well as proper back-to-basics camping, there are cabins, cottages and treehouses which take in all the joys of sleeping surrounded by nature – sitting under star-studded skies, waking up to fresh mornings with the countryside on your doorstep – and add some seriously nice comforts, such as proper duvets, hot showers and, joy of joys, posh eco loos. There are tiny homes ideal for going solo, snug boltholes built for two, and bigger places where gangs of friends can catch up around the fire or where you can rewild your kids (and let them get properly muddy). While many of these delightful lodgings are in some of the remotest places in Britain – from the Isles of Scilly in the south to the Outer Hebrides in Scotland – a handful are also fully accessible, making reconnecting with the wild easier for everyone.

These enchanting places all have a unique story to tell. There's the corner of the Lake District loved by Beatrix Potter, the island that inspired the Scouts movement, or the tiny stone turret that played a starring role in *Poldark*. Some will place you right in the heart of Britain's fascinating history – stay in homes interwoven with myths of the past, from ruined abbeys and Roman forts, or mountains where Saxon dragons roamed and the Cornish village where witches are still said to cast spells upon the sea. Many of these homes-from-home are also cared for by the National Trust. By visiting these special spots, you'll be helping the charity preserve some of our most treasured landscapes for everyone, for ever.

Above: Tan Y Bwlch cottage in Wales, with panoramic sea views from the front door.

Below: Siân exploring the South Downs Coast Path near Beachy Head.

I'm a big advocate for the joy of doing nothing and think everyone should take a leaf out of The Riverside's welcome book (page 100): 'Put the kettle on, pull up a chair, open that novel you've been meaning to read. Look out across the open fields and breathe in nature. Sometimes it's great to take your foot off the pedal and just relax.' Though if you do want to plan a mini adventure or two while you're away, you will find tips on exploring the wilderness on the doorstep. There are hiking routes, recommended cycles and swims, as well as foraging trips and other wild adventures. Most are a short walk away or reachable via public transport from each stay.

All you have to do now is decide what storybook-worthy abode you would like to escape to this weekend. A geometric tree house? A miniature castle? A cabin on a floating platform in the middle of a lake? The choice is yours – and the wild awaits.

Wild *Escapes*

1. Sally Port Cottage
2. Winnianton Farmhouse
3. Troytown Farm Campsite
4. Doyden Castle
5. Boscastle Elm Cottage
6. Brownsea Island Campsite
7. Rhossili Old Rectory
8. Tan Y Bwlch
9. Strand House
10. Lickisto Blackhouse Campsite

25. Warcleave Cottage
26. The Round House
27. Abermydyr Cottage
28. Cartref
29. The Lazy T
30. Trees
31. Faraway Treehouse
32. North Lodge
    and River Cabin

33. Bwthyn Mai
34. Hafod Y Llan
35. Dyffryn Mymbyr
36. The Lodges
    at Longshaw Estate
37. Upper Booth Campsite
38. Bird How
39. Eilean Shona
40. The Lazy Duck

11. Skoolie Stays
12. Farrs Meadow Campsite
13. Old Smock Mill
14. Chapel House Farm Campsite
15. Lyveden Cottage
16. Blacksmith's Cottage
17. Rockhouse Retreat

18. The Riverside
19. Ditchling Cabin
20. The Raft at Chigborough
21. The Boy John
22. Rose Castle Cottage
23. Low Wray Campsite
24. The Boathouse
    at Knotts End

Scotland

Northern
Ireland

England

Wales

Coast

Down to the sea

Why do we hear the call of the ocean, feel the need to be by the sea? It's a sensation that can only be described as the opposite of claustrophobia – a strong desire to look out at an empty horizon and feel the presence of an unimaginably large element, influenced endlessly by the moon.

As an island nation surrounded by an astonishing 19,491 miles of undulating coastline, it's understandable that the British are drawn to the sea. No matter where you are in the UK, the ocean is never more than 70 miles away. It is an ever-present and ever-changing enigma, from the calm, crystalline waters of the Devon Riviera to the smell of smoked kippers wafting on the Northumberland coast's breeze; from the secret smugglers' caves of Cornwall to the mysterious waters of Scapa Flow in Scotland, where everything from Viking ships to German submarines have plunged to the depths across the ages.

The UK coastline is also freely available to walkers – we can ramble over 2,700 miles of coast path (780 of which are maintained by the National Trust) or stand on over 1,500 beaches when we feel the lure of the sea. Or we can just sit at home on a stormy winter's night listening to the Shipping Forecast, read in hushed tones on Radio 4, its words a lulling rhythm – Fitzroy, Trafalgar, Sole, Lundy, Fastnet.

There must be something in these waters – the Victorians certainly thought so. Their era saw the birth of coastal tourism, as people from all walks of life flocked to sands and shingle for a 'change of air'

> The UK coastline is also freely available to walkers – we can ramble over 2,700 miles of coast path or stand on over 1,500 beaches when we feel the lure of the sea

for their physical and mental health, as well as for the good clean fun of ices, bathing huts and evening promenading. Whether you went to Bournemouth, Brighton or Blackpool (or to Queen Victoria's favourite, the Isle of Wight) on your holidays, this was a balmy, bucket-and-spade kind of British coast – now reinvented as the summer 'staycation' of today.

Tourism has replaced fishing as the main industry of many of our coastal communities, but there are still corners of the UK where nautical life prevails. In Newlyn, south-west Cornwall, crabbers, beam trawlers and potting boats come into the harbour laden with up to 40 different species of fish a day, and are operated by fishermen who can often trace their vocation back through their family for 500 years. Standing on the salt marshes of the Gower Peninsula in Wales, you can look out over an unchanged shoreline where you have a chance to spot dolphins and seals. Locals pick cockles and seaweed here, just as their ancestors did – although now with Land Rovers instead of horses and carts, and they're less likely to walk barefoot with their catch for miles, as the Gower cockle women once did to reach market.

Further west, along the coast of Pembrokeshire, renowned coastal forager, Craig Evans, forages for bounty on his local beaches: 'There are plenty of really delicious seaweeds to find in Britain. My favourite is dulse, a red seaweed that grows in long strips and which you can dry to make crisps. You can look for pepper dulse, which tastes almost like truffle, and

Above: Oystercatchers flying low over the sea surrounding Brownsea Island.

Right: Go barefoot on hundreds of beaches across the UK.

sugar kelp, which is naturally sweet. They used to call sugar kelp "poor man's weathervane" – if you hung it up outside your cottage, it would go hard in nice weather and limp when a storm was coming. Even a century ago,' Craig adds, 'people were very creative with what they foraged on the coast, often because using wild food to supplement their diet was a real necessity.'

If we once relied on the shore for sustenance, we now know how badly it needs our protection. Warming seas and rising water levels are issues affecting our coastline, as are the levels of sewage being dumped on our beaches and discarded plastic finding its way into every nook and cranny of coastal life. On UK beaches today, there are on average 5,000 pieces of plastic and 150 plastic bottles for each square mile. The damage ranges from the huge to the seemingly tiny, such

as nurdles. These small plastic pellets are a major environmental pollutant, and can be found on 75 per cent of British beaches. There will be less coast in need of cleaning up soon, too – our shoreline is being eaten away at a brisk pace by coastal erosion caused by climate change, destroying fragile landscapes including salt marsh, dunes, shingle and sea cliffs.

'I really don't know why it is that all of us are so committed to the sea, except I think it's because in addition to the fact that the sea changes, and the light changes, and ships change, it's because we all came from the sea,' said former US president, John F. Kennedy, in a poetic moment. As a nation both drawn to and in awe of the ocean, we must now commit to protect our coastline for the future – and enjoy its ephemeral moods in the present.

Sally Port Cottage, Cornwall

If you're dreaming of escaping to the sea, Virginia Woolf-style, you should hole up at Sally Port, a charming lighthouse-keeper's cottage forever standing guard over the Roseland Peninsula on the Cornish coast.

You're in your own little world at Sally Port – the lighthouse and cottage are reached down their own 300-yard long coastal track and are totally private with no public access. Once you arrive (and lug your bags down the track) it really is just you and the sea for the weekend.

St Anthony's is still a working lighthouse, with a signal that has revolved around its tower ever since it was first built back in 1835, to keep the ships in Carrick Roads Harbour safe. Originally, the lighthouse's friendly light in the darkness came from an ever-burning oil lamp (now it's powered by more reliable electricity). If you're thinking this lonely lighthouse looks like it's straight out of a children's story, you'd be right – St Anthony's played a starring role in Muppet-maker Jim Henson's much-loved 1980s TV show *Fraggle Rock*, as the underground home of the colourful little Fraggles.

Wild *Escapes*

The cottage is built onto the side of the working lighthouse and was once home to the keeper's assistant. Inside is surprisingly roomy and sleeps four in two bedrooms. The sitting room is bright and airy, with an electric wood burner to keep you warm on chilly evenings. The coastal-inspired bedrooms (there's a double and a twin) are painted white, with big,

> **Hearing the lighthouse boom out into the night is rather cosy – a feeling akin to listening to the Shipping Forecast on the radio when the rain is lashing down outside**

knitted throws on the beds and prints of the seaside villages of Padstow and St Mawes on the walls. There are sweeping ocean views from almost every window, so you can keep an eye on the waves even when you're in the bath.

Be warned before you stay here – in misty conditions the lighthouse still sounds an audible fog-bell to warn ships of the perilous coast nearby. But perhaps hearing the lighthouse boom out into the night is rather cosy – a feeling akin to listening to the Shipping Forecast on the radio when the rain is lashing down outside.

If a storm is brewing, curl up in the cottage's observation room, which has a big picture window overlooking the waves, and binoculars for checking what the local sea birds are up to. In brighter weather, the cottage also has a patio perfect for watching the tide roll in with a cup of coffee in the morning, or out again with a glass of wine at sundown.

It's tempting never to want to leave your ocean eyrie at Sally Port, but if you do, don't forget your hiking boots – the South West Coast Path runs past the top of the lighthouse's track. The main difficulty is deciding which way to go – the trail leads temptingly towards the seafood shacks of St Mawes to the right, or to the fishing village of Portscatho and the sandy cove at Porthcurnick Beach to the left. After a day of beachcombing among the coastal crowds, you can escape back to your hidden cliffside bolthole. See you down at Fraggle Rock.

On the doorstep

A foodie hike along the coast path: Follow the South West Coast Path towards Portscatho (4½ miles/1½ hours from Sally Port) and stop for lunch at the Hidden Hut, a wooden shack tucked away above Porthcurnick Beach, which serves up delicious freshly cooked local produce. Or, book in for one of the Hut's summer feast nights, held on the sands below – the lobster and chips night is a highlight.

Wild *Escapes*

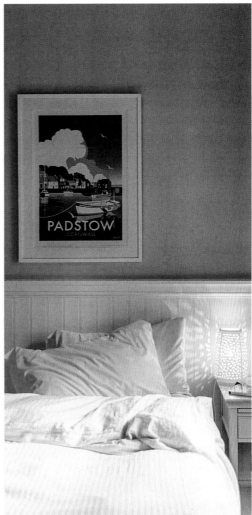

Opposite: Looking out towards Falmouth from the coastal path.

Above left: Sally Port Lighthouse at dusk. The cottage sits just behind the lighthouse.

Above right: The coastal-inspired master bedroom.

Winnianton Farmhouse, Cornwall

Lovers of a good swashbuckling story will be very happy at Winnianton Farmhouse, a spacious stone cottage overlooking a slice of the Cornish coastline that's soaked in stories of shipwrecks, pirates and buried treasure.

Ready to hunt for pieces of eight? Below the farmhouse is Dollar Cove, where silver coins can sometimes be found washed up on the beach. The cove got its name, so the story goes, from the wreck of a Spanish galleon, the *San Salvador*, lost off these shores in 1669 with a precious cargo – two tonnes of silver dollar coins. Or was it? Other stories tell that the *San Salvador* was actually carrying timber when it sank beneath the waves, and that it is a second Spanish ship, the *Rio Nova*, whose booty lies on the Cornish seabed, after it was wrecked off Dollar Cove in December 1802. An inquest reported in the Sherborne *Mercury* on 17 January 1803 stated that 'the vessel was coming from Malaga with dollars, gold and silver plate and fruit. Out of 19,000 dollars on board, about 12,000 have been saved. The vessel went to pieces as soon as she struck.' If this is the true wreck of Dollar Cove, then 7,000 silver dollars sank to the bottom of the ocean – perhaps these are the shiny coins that occasionally wash up on the sands of the cove for keen-eyed beachcombers to find.

Stroll to the next cove along the coast to seek a different kind of historical treasure – at Gunwalloe, also known as Church Cove, you'll find St Winwaloe's, a medieval church sat low in the dunes and looking out to sea. Known as the Church of the Storms for its wind-swept position, St Winwaloe's was named for a 5th-century Breton saint, who is said to have founded the first church on this site. Inside is a priceless and richly coloured medieval screen salvaged from yet another wreck – the Portuguese treasure ship the *Santo António*, which ran aground at Gunwalloe on 19 January 1527. It inspired more modern-day storytelling – the team behind the BBC adaptation of Winston Graham's historical *Poldark* series of books filmed a lamp-lit, night-time shipwreck scene in the cove.

When you're back from adventuring on this wild coastline, Winnianton Farmhouse feels like a warm welcome. The sitting room is rather grand, with velvet sofas facing the fire and an invitingly plush window seat to curl up in with a good book (one from the *Poldark* series, perhaps?). The flagstone-floored kitchen centres around a large wooden island where you can prepare dinner before serving it in the dining room, which has its own wood burner to banish the nip of winter weather. Three bedrooms are painted white and look out at the sea, the surrounding fields and the garden, where there's a big wooden table to gather around for breakfast in the sunshine while you plot your piratical adventures for the day. It's easy to go exploring on foot – the South West Coast Path runs right past the farmhouse, leading north to the reliable surfing swell of Porthleven and south to the sheltered harbour of Mullion, a safe haven for the ships that have sailed this dramatic coastline for centuries.

> If this is the true wreck of Dollar Cove, then 7,000 silver dollars sank to the bottom of the ocean – perhaps these are the shiny coins that occasionally wash up on the sands of the cove

Top: A lone surfer catches
the swell at Dollar Cove.

Bottom: Cosy living room
at Winnianton Farmhouse.

Opposite: Dollar Cove beach
at sunset. Winnianton Farmhouse
sits just behind the cove.

On the doorstep

Visit Britain's most southerly point: Lizard Point is a wild and windswept spot where you may see glossy bottlenose dolphins leaping above the waves from the Lizard Lighthouse, a 20-minute drive or 3-hour walk from Winnianton Farmhouse.

Kynance Cove: A 7-mile/2½-hour stroll from the farmhouse along the South West Coast Path leads you to the rocky expanse of Kynance Cove. A 'beach for the adventurous', Kynance's pure white stretch of sand, studded with tall rock stacks, is often listed among the most beautiful beaches in the world.

Wild *Escapes*

Troytown Farm Campsite, Isles of Scilly

If you are picturing waking up, unzipping your tent and jumping straight into the ocean, set up camp at Troytown Farm. Life goes at a slow pace on the car-free island of St Agnes, one of the Isles of Scilly found 28 miles off the Cornish coast. This grassy camping meadow, with views of the Atlantic from your tent door, is a wonderful place to take things down a notch.

If you are not familiar with the subtropical Scilly archipelago, you are in for a treat. Reached by boat or tiny prop plane from Newquay (and from Exeter airport between spring and autumn), this scattering of five inhabited islands feels a world apart from the mainland. Journey from the largest island, St Mary's, to the four car-free 'off islands' by boat to find white sand beaches, secret gardens, flower farms and coastal pubs.

Each island is unique and well worth exploring, but St Agnes is a bit extra special. The most remote and south-westerly of the islands, this is England's final frontier – and you can camp right on its edge. Troytown Farm campsite is in some ways a simple camping spot, with two large meadows and washing facilities, including hot showers. The jaw-dropping part is the location – the fields run gently down to meet the Atlantic, with views of sparkling sea, Bishop Rock Lighthouse, the rugged western rocks and the uninhabited island of Annet right in front of your pitch. Two bell tents are available if you don't want to lug your tent to the islands, but if you do bring lots of kit, the campsite will send their tractor and trailer to collect you from the harbour when you arrive.

The fields run gently down to meet the Atlantic, with views of sparkling sea, Bishop Rock Lighthouse, the rugged western rocks and the uninhabited island of Annet right in front of your pitch

Ready to meet your camping neighbours? Nine milking cows (Shamrock, Sundance, Rose, Honey, Westie, Sunset, Cilla, Humbug and Humble, if you want to be on first-name terms) also call this working dairy farm home. The farm shop is open daily, selling fresh, home-produced milk, butter, sausages and burgers. There's also that quintessential summer delight: an ice cream shop selling homemade treats. The clotted cream ice cream is legendary, and the sorbet flavoured with roses picked on the island is pretty special too.

Kids (along with cows and grown-ups) run free range here – with no cars on the dirt roads, there's room to play. Buckets, spades, shrimping nets and crabbing lines are available to borrow from Troytown; hammocks are strung up from the rocks. Right next door is Periglis Beach where, in the summer months, you'll find St Agnes Watersports set up under a canopy. They rent out kayaks and stand-up paddleboards, so you can go paddling along the island's edge. On calm days, pack a picnic and paddle across to the uninhabited beaches on the surrounding islets. Back on St Agnes, campfires are permitted on the beach – a great place to sit as night falls, as the lack of light pollution on the Scillies means incredible views of the Milky Way and dazzling displays of shooting stars. Sitting here as the sun turns the water gold is a simple pleasure – just like everything else at Troytown.

On the doorstep

Kayak to the pub: Rent a kayak from St Agnes Watersports on the beach below the campsite and paddle the island's shoreline clockwise to moor up at The Turk's Head, the island's only pub, for a drink with a view of the sea.

Walk to Gugh: This tiny island is connected to St Agnes by a sandbar. Walk here at low tide (a 6-mile/2-hour circuit takes in both islands) to visit the Old Man of Gugh, a Bronze Age standing stone, and to go for a dip at the lovely sandbar 'beach' that appears at low tide. Be sure to check tide times before you set out, though – Gugh is cut off at high tide.

Wild *Escapes*

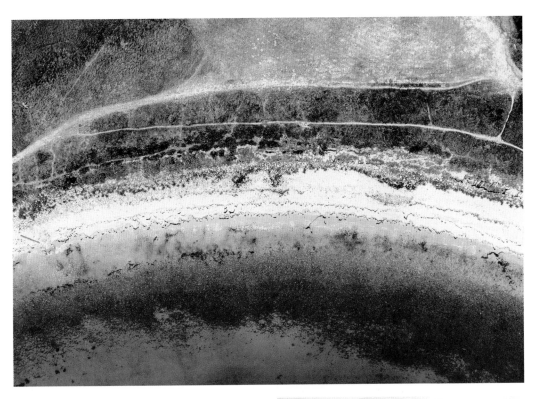

Left: Pitch up at Troytown right on the island shore.

Top: Aerial view of white sand cove on St. Agnes, one of many idyllic beaches on the island.

Right: Kayaks and canoes on the beach next to Troytown, ready for exploring the coves and surrounding islands.

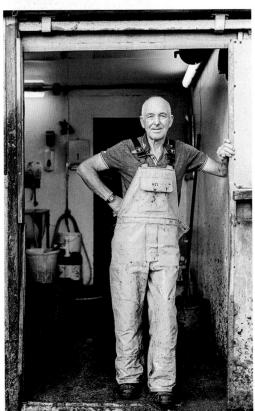

As well as a campsite, Troytown is also a working dairy farm. Tim the farmer milks the cows on site every morning and produces delicious, award-winning ice cream, available at the campsite's ice cream parlour.

Doyden Castle, Cornwall

Be queen or king of all you survey at Doyden Castle. A fortress in miniature, this neo-Gothic folly on the Cornish coast was constructed in the 1830s by wealthy bon viveur Samuel Symons; not for military defence, but as a place to entertain his friends, who spent their time merry-making by the sea. Bequeathed to the National Trust in 1956, Doyden has been transformed from a gambler's den into a plush hideaway, with endless views out to the Atlantic from its own grassy bluff.

This tiny castle-turned-holiday home still feels delightfully luxurious inside, and has a glamorous double life as a TV star, too. Nearby Port Isaac is the fishing village used as a backdrop for British medical comedy drama *Doc Martin*, and fans of the good doctor will recognise this tower – it plays a starring role in series five. The castle was also the home of another medic – Dr Dwight Enys – in the 1970s TV adaptation of swashbuckling Cornish romance series, *Poldark*.

Inside this little eyrie is the perfect space for two to share. Through the arched stone doorway is a sitting room with a wood burner to warm the room in winter, and a dining nook surrounded by mullioned windows. Upstairs there's a real sense of

> The double bedroom's windows look out at the ever-changing blue hues of ocean and sky, and kestrels often fly past the tower while making their rounds of the cliffs

space and sea – the double bedroom's windows look out at the ever-changing blue hues of ocean and sky, and kestrels often fly past the tower while making their rounds of the cliffs. Thick velvet curtains and an intricate metal headboard make this feel as if you're staying in a pocket-sized medieval castle.

This little fortress sits on the South West Coast Path, so you can explore the edge of Cornwall in both directions. Other hikers may walk right past the cottage, so you won't feel fully isolated in your stronghold – join them on foot to hike east towards Tintagel, where King Arthur is said to have been born, or west towards the fishing port of Padstow's smart foodie scene. You're also next to a remnant of Cornwall's chequered mining history – the fenced-off open shaft of Doyden Point mine, once explored for silver-lead and copper, is next to the tower, and the coast path now runs through the site of the mine's horse whim (a device similar to a windlass, used to haul materials to the surface).

Make sure you're back at your Bacchanalian hideaway while the light lasts – the best time of day here is the golden hour, when the sun sets low over the Atlantic and you can sit outside Doyden and be ruler of your own seaside citadel.

TO
COASTAL
FOOTPATH

On the doorstep

Take to the water: Cornish Rock Tors, a fish cellar-turned-watersports centre, takes adventurers on kayaking and stand-up paddleboarding trips from the peaceful cove of Port Gaverne. A 4-mile/1¾-hour coastal walk from the Castle; this small harbour is also a calm place to swim.

Hike the South West Coast Path: Once used by coastguards to keep an eye out for smugglers, the South West Coast Path (all uninterrupted 630 miles of it) stretches from Minehead in Somerset to Poole Harbour in Dorset, passing through Devon and Cornwall along the way. You'll need seven weeks to tackle the whole length of this easy-to-navigate trail, or dip in for just a day or two of walking.

Opposite left (top to bottom): Sea views from inside the castle. The coastal path runs past the front door.

Opposite right: Paddleboarders set off from Port Quin village.

Below: The interiors are a luxurious mix of traditional and cosy.

Boscastle Elm Cottage, Cornwall

It's always witching hour in Boscastle, a spookily charming fishing village tucked out of sight on the north Cornish coast. Three rivers come together in a deep valley, which shelters the clustered village set on their banks, where an Elizabethan harbour leads out to the wild Cornish sea. Boscastle has been an important natural harbour since the 12th century, when clever local witches used to sell 'wind' in the form of magical knotted ropes to the captains of becalmed ships waiting in the harbour for better sailing weather. They say there's still a coven of witches in the village today – you can learn more about their foremothers at the village's fascinating Museum of Witchcraft and Magic (more of which later), and even go searching for the devil that lives in the harbour on a coastal walk.

> **Local witches used to sell 'wind' in the form of magical knotted ropes to the captains of becalmed ships waiting in the harbour for better sailing weather**

Wherever you explore, enchantment is weaved into the very stone and mortar of Boscastle. The village's narrow cobbled alleyways are often busy with visitors in the summer months – but the good news is that you can escape a mile upstream on the River Valency to a picture-perfect 17th-century cottage, camouflaged in the trees of the Valency Valley, for some peace and quiet. Elm Cottage would make a brilliant stand-in as the witches' cottage from Hansel and Gretel – you'll find this unspoilt little house down a steep and narrow forest lane, with a wooden gate leading invitingly into a postage stamp-sized front garden. Inside, there's a surprisingly airy dining room, a well-equipped kitchen with a flagstone floor and a bright sitting room with a wood burner (burning pesky children not recommended).

Upstairs, watch your head on the low-slung beams in the two charming bedrooms with patchwork quilts and windows overlooking the back garden, which holds a picnic table for al fresco suppers. What you won't find at Elm Cottage is a Wi-Fi connection or mobile phone signal – consider this a much-needed unplugged retreat.

A 20-minute walk from the cottage down to the harbourside in Boscastle leads you past a bustling book exchange, The Rocket Store (impossible to pass by without sampling one of their local seafood dishes) and the Museum of Witchcraft and Magic, a must for the curious of mind. It's easy to lose yourself completely in the narrow corridors of this small but crammed museum, which leads you through the weird and wonderful history of the occult. Beginning with the apparatus used to torture medieval enchantresses, the collection also includes a re-creation of a wise woman's cottage, displays of herbal ointments and potions and some rather unusual keepsakes (don't miss the pickled two-headed piglet). The final display covers the rites and rituals of modern-day Wiccans.

It wouldn't be a weekend in Cornwall without swapping civilisation (and possible conjurors) for the great outdoors. Boscastle's coastline is its crowning glory, rising up in high cliffs on both sides of the water. Hike up to the left and you can tramp all the way to Tintagel. Beyond it are lesser-visited coves perfect for wild swimming. You may even catch a glimpse of the devil himself as you hike – legend has it he sends out streams of foam from a blow-hole known as the Devil's Bellows when the tide is right.

On the doorstep

A witchy walk: A 9-mile/3-hour circular walk from Boscastle will take you along the coast path south to Tintagel, believed to have been King Arthur's stronghold, where you can explore ruins on the cliffs and search for Merlin's Cave on the beach below. Then head across fields to St Nectan's Glen, where there's a spectacular waterfall and a pagan shrine to discover, and Rocky Valley, to seek out ancient maze-like stone carvings in the rocks.

Surf the Cornish coast: A 25-minute drive north of Boscastle is the seaside surf mecca of Bude, where you can catch a wave or two with the locals if you bring your own board or book a surfing lesson with the Big Blue Surf School, based on Summerleaze Beach.

Opposite: Boscastle Cottage nestled in the woodland.

Above (left to right): Views out to sea from Boscastle village. Visit the Museum of Witchcraft and Magic. Curl up in the cosy rocking chair nook inside the cottage.

Bottom: The harbour at low tide in the early morning light.

Wild *Escapes*

Brownsea Island Campsite, Dorset

Ready your flags, badges and three-fingered salute – the island that inspired Robert Baden-Powell to start the Scouting and Guiding movement still has an adventurous spirit today. Brownsea Island sits in the calm waters of Poole Harbour, but despite its proximity to Dorset on the mainland, this little area of land has a wild spirit, a flourishing wildlife population and a wonderful campsite from which to explore, only recently opened to the public.

Brownsea isn't big – it's just 1½ miles long and three-quarters of a mile wide – but it's home to a surprising array of wildlife habitats. A mix of woodland, heathland and a lagoon create a haven for birds and mammals, and the most famous resident is the red squirrel – a population of 200 thrive on Brownsea. You're likely to see their curious faces, topped with two tufty ears, peeking out at you from behind a tree on one of the many walking paths that criss-cross this car-free island. If you're a keen birdwatcher, the lagoon and wetlands is something of a stop-off for migrating birds, including sandwich terns and oystercatchers, and you may catch the electric blue flash of a kingfisher hunting in the shallows. Come nightfall, Brownsea's birds change shifts with bats silhouetted against the stars – the light pollution-free night sky is glorious here.

If this all seems like a scene straight out of a Famous Five book, you'd be correct. Enid Blyton set *Five on Whispering Island* on Brownsea, although the island is better known as the birthplace of the Scouting and Guiding movement. In 1907, Lord Baden-Powell brought a group of 20 local children here to take part in an experimental camp, living close to nature and learning practical skills. It launched a global movement, and now Scout groups from 75 countries visit the island annually. For years, only Scouts and Guides could camp here – the island was only opened to the public in 1963, and to campers in 2018.

To reach Brownsea to camp, first, hop on the foot ferry that runs daily from Poole Harbour to Brownsea, or book the wheelchair-friendly Seahorse ferry. You'll be met on the pier, given a map of the island and sent on a 20-minute walk to find the campsite. It's a bit of a treasure hunt to get here – but one that rewards you with a real sense of escape.

Bring your own tent to pitch in this shady woodland glade, or if you fancy something special, book one of the campsite's tree tents, which hang between the branches to create a suspended platform with a tented roof. They're great for stargazing and feeling totally immersed in nature.. The practical bits – the campsite has hot showers, washing-up stations and a communal dining area that's sheltered from the rain. Or, if you're in a group and like the idea of a roof over your head, rent South Shore Lodge, a lovely Victorian gamekeeper's house with a private garden leading to the sea and bunkhouse accommodation for 12 guests. South Shore Lodge is open year-round, so if you want to feel like you've got the island all to yourself, this is a great out-of-season stay. The south-facing beach and warm, shallow water right in front of the Lodge make for the perfect swim spot, too.

> A mix of woodland, heathland and a lagoon create a haven for birds and mammals, and the most famous resident is the red squirrel – a population of 200 thrive on Brownsea

On the doorstep

Kayak to the island: Brownsea is reachable by kayak or canoe from the mainland (dependant on the tides) and packing a tent and crossing to South Shore makes for the perfect canoe camping expedition if you're a proficient paddler. It's a 3-mile/1–2-hour journey from Poole Harbour, and a landing fee is payable on the island. Make sure to book your pitch before you set off.

Supper and safari: Time your camping trip to coincide with a seasonal event. Join the rangers of the National Trust and Dorset Wildlife Trust for an evening exploring the island's habitats with the experts. You'll learn more about birdcalls and spot the elusive nocturnal nightjars who flock here in summer on their Brownsea Supper and Safari tour, which also includes dinner in the island's café.

Islands surrounding Brownsea, with the mainland in the distance.

Wild *Escapes*

(top to bottom, left to right): Looking out from inside one of the island's bell tents. Peacocks roam the campsite. Wooden signs name all the global scout groups who have stayed at Brownsea campsite. The bell tents all have colourful, cosy interiors.

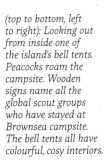

Wild *Escapes*

Rhossili Old Rectory, Gower Peninsula

'Gower is a very beautiful peninsula, some miles from this blowsy town ... As a matter of fact it is one of the loveliest sea-coast stretches in the whole of Britain', wrote Dylan Thomas of this small but perfect peninsula. Gower isn't huge – just 70 square miles in size, bound by the Loughor Estuary to the north and Swansea Bay to the east. Yet between its shores are fairytale woods, sleepy moorland villages and one of the most beautiful stretches of beach in Britain – Rhossili Bay.

At three miles long, Rhossili is a vast stretch of sand, backed by steep hills and looking out at the green headland of Worm's Head. The bay is regularly named the most beautiful beach in Britain, but it's often surprisingly quiet outside of hot summer weekends. At dusk and dawn, it can feel totally empty and remote – except for one solitary cottage, perched high above the sands in splendid isolation and keeping a watchful eye on the rolling sea. This is Rhossili Old Rectory, an elegant National Trust cottage that makes the perfect place to escape to if you're itching for a real sense of space.

The house has had a rather fascinating past since it was first built in the 1800s to house the local rector. It was used as a radar centre during the Second World War and has even played a starring role in the BBC's sci-fi series *Torchwood*. Now it's a lofty retreat for larger groups, sleeping seven with a front-row seat over Rhossili.

> **At dusk and dawn, the beach can feel totally empty and remote – except for one solitary cottage, perched high above the sands in splendid isolation**

Rhossili Old Rectory is reached down a bumpy, grassy track past grazing sheep that cling to the cliffside. The house is at the end of the road, but there's a steep, narrow path leading straight down to the beach, and the Wales Coast Path continues on past the house towards Llangennith. It's a wild and windswept spot, but inside the Rectory is surprisingly comfortable and cosy. A wood burner warms the sitting room in winter, while in summer you can breakfast outside on the lawn and toast the ocean. A separate snug makes a lovely spot for a bit of peace and quiet with a good book. Upstairs are four airy bedrooms (one twin, two doubles and one single) with solid iron bedsteads, picture windows looking out to sea and calm, white colour schemes, plus two modern bathrooms.

The view from the cottage must be one of the most enticing in Britain – it'll have you itching to grab your hiking boots (or your wetsuit). Out past the rolling tide, often scattered with surfers, looms Worm's Head. So named because Viking invaders thought it resembled a serpent or dragon (or 'wrym' in Old Norse) rising from the depths. This rocky island is cut off from the mainland at high tide, but when the tide is right you can walk down the causeway and onto what feels like the edge of the world. It makes a great short walk from the cottage, and you'll be following in literary footsteps – Dylan Thomas wrote that he would often tramp on the cliffs around Worm's Head, 'taking my devils for an airing'.

On the doorstep

Walk from Penmaen to Rhossili on the Gower Way: The Gower Way, a 35-mile route that winds its way from Rhossili to upland Mawr, meanders through some of the richest history and wildest coastline of the peninsula. Catch a bus to Penmaen to tackle the 8-mile/4½-hour stretch back to Rhossili, passing the golden sandy stretches of Oxwich Bay and Three Cliffs Bay before you end up at the Worm's Head Hotel, where you can warm up by the fire.

Explore Weobley Castle: The very definition of a romantic ruin, perched on the edge of the salt marsh a 15-minute drive from Rhossili. Knock on the door of the farmhouse on the edge of the castle's land and they'll sell you a ticket (plus a shank of salt marsh lamb if the fancy takes you) and leave you free to wander all over this 14th-century castle, once home to the Lords of Gower.

Above: Bikes on the costal path behind Rhossili beach.

Below: Looking back at Rhossili Old Rectory from the beach.

Wild Escapes

Top left: Cliffs leading to Worm's Head.

Top right: Stylishly modern interiors inside the cottage.

Bottom: Sunset between the Helvetia shipwreck on Rhossili Beach.

Tan Y Bwlch, Gwynedd

If you must go down to the sea again, to the call of the running tide – stay at Tan Y Bwlch, a Welsh cottage with doors and windows full to bursting with all the colours of the ocean. The name of this Grade II-listed cottage means 'under the pass' in Welsh, but perhaps uwchben y mor – or 'above the sea' – might have been a neater fit. Here you are on one of the fingertips of 'Eryri's arm'; the wild Llŷn Peninsula extends 30 miles into the Irish Sea from north-west Wales, south of the Isle of Anglesey. Right below the cottage is the half-moon sweep of Porth Neigwl (Hell's Mouth) beach, lapped by the Irish Sea, a crystalline-blue on clear days and darker iron hue when the sky is overcast. So called because it offered precious little shelter for sailors, Hell's Mouth is now known as a more heavenly spot for beach-goers and surfers, although swimmers should be aware of the strong currents that nip at the sands here.

If a storm does threaten, wind your way back to Tan Y Bwlch along the coast path. The inside of this traditional Penllyn 'crog' cottage ticks all the cosy boxes – inglenook fireplace, wooden floors, piles of Welsh blankets and beams dating back to when the cottage was first built in the 19th century. Turn your back on the sea views and you'll find a sitting room with a wood burner and an old ornamental bread oven still built into the wall, plus a kitchen painted white and stocked with patterned

So-called because it offered precious little shelter for sailors, Hell's Mouth is now known as a more heavenly spot for beach-goers and surfers

china. A staircase from the sitting room leads to the original crog (or loft) bedroom, topped and tailed by a solid oak floor and hefty beams. This double room feels cheery thanks to the bright geometric Welsh blankets – these designs date back to when sheep farming began in Wales. Textile production was at the heart of Welsh village life for centuries, taking place in cottages just like this one; at Tan Y Bwlch, you'll snuggle up under a traditional Caernarfon, or 'portcullis' design, a repeated series of pixilated squares, spikes and dots in contrasting colours that will brighten up the rainiest day.

You don't need to go far to be immersed in more colour – the cottage is in the grounds of the National Trust's Plas yn Rhiw estate. Lovingly restored by the Keating sisters in the 1930s, the crowning glory of this 17th-century manor house is the acres of lush gardens that Welsh architect Sir Clough Williams-Ellis described as 'a blossoming jungle of fuchsias, figs and azaleas'. It's also home to an orchard of Welsh apple trees, a wildflower meadow and a woodland carpeted in snowdrops in spring, and all just a few steps from Tan Y Bwlch. Everywhere you explore here, the ocean fills your eyes and ears. If you're feeling in need of a big dose of fresh sea air, this cockle-warming cottage is the ultimate hidey-hole.

On the doorstep

Abersoch Beach and Bardsey Island: This ever-popular stretch of sand, a 20-minute drive or a 2-hour walk from Tan Y Bwlch, is a classic for bucket-and-spade days out. Abersoch is lined by brightly painted beach huts and has safe, sheltered water to paddle in. You can also catch a boat from here to Bardsey Island, a storied place known as the 'island of 20,000 saints'. Hike up the island's own Marilyn-sized hill (over 150m / 492ft), Mynydd Enlli – a 3-mile/2-hour circular walk – for views back to the mainland.

Portmeirion: A 45-minute drive along the wild Snowdonia coast brings you to this beautiful and sometimes bizarre village, a pastel-coloured creation born of one man's love of Italianate architecture. Sir Clough Williams-Ellis's 20th-century vision is now open to the public, who can wander among its hodgepodge of colourful *trompe l'oeil* houses.

Opposite: Tan Y Bwlch looks out onto views of Porth Neigwl Bay.

Top: Aberdaron village, a short drive from the cottage.

Left to right: The cottage at dusk. The cosy living room with inglenook fireplace.

Strand House, County Antrim

Fáilte go Cushendun (or 'Welcome to Cushendun' in English). The charm of this seaside village on Northern Ireland's north coast is likely to stay with you forever. In the heart of the Antrim coastline and Glens Area of Outstanding Natural Beauty, Cushendun (from the Irish Cois Abhann Duinne, meaning 'beside the River Dun') looks curiously different to its surrounding fishing communities – this grand stretch of white terraced houses was built in the Cornish style in 1912 by Baron Cushendun, in an attempt to please his Cornish-born wife, who missed her home back in Penzance. Designed by architect Clough Williams-Ellis in 1912 (yes, he of Portmeirion-building fame, see page 48), the village looks out over a neat harbour where red and blue boats bob, and at the sickle-shaped sandy stretch of Cushendun beach. The estate has been cared for by the National Trust since 1945.

Look out to sea and on clear days you can see the Mull of Kintyre in Scotland, only about 15 miles away across the North Channel. Follow the gorse-lined beach a few hundred yards north from the car park and you'll come across a white doll's house of a cottage on the edge of the village, its windows and doors painted a cheerful cherry red. This is Strand House, just steps from the sand. Downstairs is a higgledy-piggledy layout of rooms. A sitting room in neutral sand tones

> **The village looks out over a neat harbour where red and blue boats bob, and at the sickle-shaped sandy stretch of Cushendun beach**

has one red-framed window looking out to sea and the other back to Cushendun, plus a wood burner to stoke when the mercury drops. Three warm, wood-floored bedrooms await upstairs – there's a roomy double, one twin and one tiny single room that's mostly taken up by a big window, so you can tuck yourself in and watch the sky darken over the sea as you fall asleep.

You may recognise the dramatic landscape of the Antrim coast surrounding the cottage from the *Game of Thrones* TV series, where it played a starring role as the weather-beaten fictional landscape of Stormlands (ruled by House Baratheon). If it does pelt down with rain, you can escape to the fireside at Mary McBride's pub, a local institution much-loved for its hearty home-cooked food and pints of Guinness served by the stove. Once the smallest pub in Ireland, there's more elbow room at Mary's these days – and on summer evenings you may share a corner of the bar with a gaggle of fiddlers playing lively traditional Irish tunes.

There are some other locals you should meet nearby, too. Grand Glenmona House, also commissioned by Baron Cushendun, is now a haven for bright-eyed and bushy-tailed red squirrels, which build nests in the surrounding conifers and peep curiously down at visitors to this unspoilt place.

Left: Dare to cross the bridge at nearby Carrick-a-Rede.
Below: Strand House sits right on the beach front.
Opposite: Looking towards Cushendun village from the beach at Strand House.

Wild *Escapes*

On the doorstep

Giant's Causeway: A 40-minute drive from Cushendun, Giant's Causeway needs no introduction – it's been sought out by visitors to Northern Ireland for centuries. Was this crazy jumble of ballast columns rising from the ocean caused by cooling lava 60 million years ago – or by angry giant Fionn mac Cumhaill? The jury is out, but whether geology or folklore gets your vote, the Giant's Causeway is a humbling sight. It's 5-mile/3½-hour (including a stop) circular trail is a great way to explore it on foot.

Drive Northern Ireland's Coastal Causeway route: Take this scenic seaside route from Cushendun onwards to Londonderry (Derry) to explore dramatic Ballintoy harbour, another *Game of Thrones* filming location (as Lordsport, the main port of Pyke), and onwards to visit the Giant's Causeway, the ruins of Dunluce Castle, clinging to the cliffside, and to tackle hiking routes in the Mourne Mountains.

Lickisto Blackhouse Camping, Lewis and Harris

Was there ever a wilder place in Britain than Lewis and Harris? One island with a name that sounds like two, this landmass is the biggest of the string of islands that make up Scotland's Outer Hebrides archipelago. It really feels like you're at the edge of everything here on the west coast; the only thing between you and Greenland is the Atlantic, and these twinned lands hold many treasures, from ancient standing stones to white sand beaches that rival the tropics, plus a buzzing arts community and even a gin distillery.

People have lived on Lewis and Harris since around 8500 BC, and the Norse influence here dates back to the 9th century, when Viking raiders arrived. It's a land that still feels steeped in history everywhere you walk. At Lickisto Blackhouse Camping, you're up close to how life used to be for the island communities that farmed this challenging but beautiful terrain.

If you've never heard of a blackhouse before, here's your potted history lesson: they're traditional, low-slung dwellings found in the Hebrides, built with dry-stone walls packed with earth and covered with a thatch of turf. Smoke escapes from the cooking fire through the turf, rather than through a chimney, lending the houses the sooty, dark appearance from which their name is derived. Blackhouses were in use on the island until the 1970s, but many are now in disrepair. Gearrannan Blackhouse Village on Lewis is a living museum, and a good place to learn more about how these houses were used.

This bohemian campsite on the rocky shore of South Harris is built around a well-cared-for, 150-year-old blackhouse, which is now a sort of common room for visitors who pass through here, offering a snug sitting room where campers can chill out, chat and peruse the book collection, as well as hot showers and a kitchen. Or, if you don't fancy cooking, join one of Lickisto's regular themed feast nights, where you can enjoy curries, tacos or Scottish stews. Saturday nights are music nights – fiddle, anyone? – and the Drift In Shop stocks locally-made crafts, as well as fresh veggies grown in the campsite's polytunnel.

> **It really feels like you're at the edge of everything here on the west coast; the only thing between you and Greenland is the Atlantic**

If you fancy something a little more unusual than your trusty tent, the campsite has a clutch of yurts as well as a Bedouin tent and a hobbit-style wooden bothy, all of which make wonderfully cosy places to escape the weather (their wood burners come in handy for drying your socks if you get caught in the good old Scottish mizzle). This isn't luxury glamping though – like everything on the Isle of Lewis and Harris, Lickisto is a little licked by the elements, and is more rugged retreat than glam hideaway.

Campers and campervans are both welcome at Lickisto, and you can choose to pitch up with a view of the sea from your tent door or to plump for a more sheltered space in woodland. Bring your binoculars – seals, otters and golden eagles are all regular visitors to the sea loch that laps against the rocks at the bottom of the campsite. You can also explore further into the loch on calm weather days with a kayak or stand-up paddleboard – Lickisto has a few available to hire. Come nightfall, the campsite is sometimes visited by an elusive and exciting special guest – the Northern Lights can occasionally be seen dancing in the sky above.

On the doorstep

Calanais Standing Stones: Humans have lived on these islands for over 9,000 years. These eerily beautiful standing stones, which visitors are free to walk around, remain as a sign of lives lived long ago. The exact purpose of the stones is unknown but imagining these ancient peoples at this very spot is half the fun.

Hike Ceapabhal and Scarista Beach: You'd be forgiven for thinking the white sands and clear turquoise waters of Scarista were in the Caribbean – until you dip a toe in the icy sea, that is. A 5-mile/3-hour hike up Ceapabhal mountain is a great way to blow away the cobwebs before visiting gorgeous Scarista beach on South Harris. Keep your eyes peeled for the Isle of Skye and even distant St Kilda on a clear day, a wild UNESCO-listed archipelago on the very tip of Britain.

Above: Relax outside the yurts with views of the bay.

Opposite left: The rustic communal living area at Blackhouse Campsite.

Opposite bottom left: Each camping pitch has its own name, relating to aspects of life and nature on Harris.

Meadows

Magical meadows

Hay rattle, meadow saxifrage, wood cranesbill. Butterfly orchid, ragged robin, meadowsweet. Oxeye daisies, Yorkshire fog, the melancholy thistle. Naming the lyrical plants and flowers found in Britain's wildflower meadows is like reading a poem.

Our meadows don't often get the same attention that the UK's lofty mountain peaks or glittering coastline, and while we're good at shouting about the need to fix our fells and sort out sea sewage, managing grasslands and meadows isn't usually big in the news. But our flower- and wildlife-rich grasslands deserve to be venerated – they are one of the UK's most precious landscapes, providing vital habitats for birds and mammals, bees and butterflies, and creating a home for up to 40 plant species per square metre.

Now here's a sombre fact you may not know – as a nation we have lost 97 per cent (that's almost 6.4 million hectares) of our wildflower meadows since the 1930s. After the Second World War, the intensification of farming resulted in a massive decline in hay meadows and the plant and animal species that they support. In a drive to produce more food, chemical fertilisers and fast-growing grasses were introduced, and native grasses and wild flowers simply could not compete. This vanishing has led some species, such as the large blue butterfly, the turtle dove and the shrill carder bee, to the brink of extinction (the charming turtle dove alone has declined by 98 per cent since the 1970s). Fifty bee species in the UK are in decline, and two have disappeared completely.

Meadows don't just provide an essential home to wild things – they're a secret weapon against our environmental crisis, too. Meadows prevent flooding, combating climate change. They store and clean rain water, and they capture carbon. Combined with forests, they're the Earth's own efficient green pair of lungs.

They are also truly ancient landscapes. Our island has been the 'green and pleasant land' of William Blake's 'Jerusalem' since Neolithic times, when forests were felled and haymaking began. By the Middle Ages, the Domesday book recorded meadows all across the country, but today only around 1,000 hectares (2,470 acres) of traditional upland hay meadows and 1,500 hectares (3,700 acres) of lowland meadows remain – places where you can still hear the hum of bees, see swallows skimming across the fields or spot the tall ears of a hare among flower heads.

Many organisations are working to bring back the wildflower meadows we've lost, such as the National Trust's Making Meadows appeal. Donations are helping restore meadowland at Trust places, where flower seeds are being busily sown on 1,000 hectares (247 acres) of new and restored meadowland. And the good news is that swathes of meadow and pockets of wildflowers are springing up again on farms and in parks across Britain. Local councils now leave wildflowers to flourish where they would once have been mown, letting poppies and oxeye daisies take over roundabouts and ancient

> **Meadows don't just provide an essential home to wild things – they're a secret weapon against our environmental crisis, too**

Left: Cowslips cover the meadows at Lyveden in spring.

Below: Buttercups are a cheerful sight in any wildflower meadow.

herbs grow in public parks, while home gardeners (who now provide an essential source of nectar to bees and other pollinators) are learning to embrace daisies and clover on their lawns and to encourage wildflowers back to our gardens. That's what you call a grassroots movement.

Meadows aren't just important – they are a simple pleasure, too. 'Among the meadow hay cocks / 'Tis beautiful to lie / When pleasantly the day looks / And gold like is the sky,' wrote the Victorian poet John Clare in 'Haymaking'. Walking in meadows on a sunny spring day when poppies and cornflowers bloom is one of life's joys, and there are easy ways to appreciate them without impacting their biodiversity, such as following established footpaths and the field boundaries to avoid trampling rare plants or stepping on hidden bird's nests.

Make hay while the sun shines by visiting, enjoying and helping to protect our astonishingly beautiful wild grasslands, then by growing your own clutch of wildflowers at home.

Wild *Escapes*

Skoolie Stays, West Sussex

All aboard Skoolie – this magic yellow school bus may not travel far, but it's perfect for a glamping adventure on the South Coast. All-American Skoolie hails from Florida and travelled across the Atlantic Ocean to reach its current home, the corner of a meadow in Sussex, making for a very unique place to stay within shouting distance of the chalk cliffs of Beachy Head.

Inside, the converted school bus is surprisingly chic and spacious. The main living space is lined with warm teak, making it feel as if you're snug inside a (rather strangely proportioned) wooden cabin. There's a king-sized double bed, plus two foldaway bunks that are the perfect size for children. Little glampers will love spotting all of Skoolie's original dials, buttons and gadgets (it still has its original fold-out stop sign) and getting to sit in the driver's seat will let imaginations run wild. While Skoolie can't be hired to drive yourself, if you've got your own dream glamping spot in mind you can arrange for the bus to be dropped off at a destination of your choice for a choose-your-own bus adventure.

In the main body of the bus, there's a smart kitchenette equipped with everything you might need to cook up a feast, plus an American diner-style sitting area – perfect for two sharing supper – and a squashy sofa facing the wood burner. There's also a tucked-away bathroom with shower and compost loo. Shelves hold more delights, such as books to borrow and games to play, including a US edition of Monopoly. In short, Skoolie's as well-kitted-out as any plush holiday cottage. Going off-grid has never looked smarter.

On sunny days, the place to be is the clever drop-down balcony at the back of the bus, where you can have a cuppa and sit with a book in the sunshine without having to get off Skoolie at all. Or set up camp outside the bus and cook up a barbeque with a view of the sea – there's a fire pit and benches looking out towards Beachy Head from the rolling meadow, which grows high with wild grasses dotted with butterflies in the summer.

Your big, yellow home-from-home is parked just a mile from Beachy Head's bright white chalk cliffs and red-striped lighthouse

Winter weekending? The log fire heats the bus up in a jiffy in cold weather, and innovative sheep's wool insulation traps warmth inside the bus brilliantly. If you love to camp in your own tent all summer, Skoolie makes for a snug alternative when the mercury drops.

Hop off the bus, and you're right by the coast. Your big, yellow home-from-home is parked just a mile from Beachy Head's bright white chalk cliffs and red-striped lighthouse, and the coast path lets you stretch your legs towards the legendary Seven Sisters cliffs, or the wide-open spaces of the South Downs. The town of Eastbourne (proudly England's sunniest spot) is next door, and buzzy Brighton is also an hour's jaunt by bus (a public one) from Beachy Head, if you're hankering for the bright lights of the city. But you may find that you want to spend most of your time on a road trip to nowhere aboard Skoolie – it really is too cool for school.

Above: Relax on the balcony of Skoolie.

Below: In the private meadow in front of the bus, a firepit is surrounded by benches, perfect for keeping warm under the stars.

Opposite: Quirky interiors of the bus, which is surprisingly spacious.

Wild *Escapes*

On the doorstep

South Downs Way: 'The Downs – too much for one pair of eyes, enough to float a whole population in happiness, if only they would look', wrote Virginia Woolf. Go looking yourself along the South Downs Way, with 99 miles of chalky walking paths, grassy headland and sparkling sea views. The most challenging, but arguably most beautiful section is Seven Sisters and Birling Gap – a series of chalk sea cliffs that will bring you right back to Skoolie.

Cuckmere Haven: Loved by everyone from Charles Dickens, who lived here, to Queen Victoria, who liked a stroll on its pebbles, the spot where the river Cuckmere meets the sea in the shadow of the Seven Sisters is a wonderful place to get a big dose of sea air, or to join local painters and photographers by capturing its beauty.

A short walk from the bus and you are at the South Downs National Park white cliffs. Look down to sea and you'll spot the Beachy Head lighthouse.

Farrs Meadow Campsite, Dorset

Anyone who's nostalgic for old-fashioned camping trips from childhood summers gone by should spend a night under canvas at Farrs Meadow. A handful of tents are scattered across a bucolic meadow surrounded by shady woodland at this Dorset campsite, where wild swimmers can blow the cobwebs away with a morning dip in the River Stour.

Campsites often come with bells, whistles and a big dose of mod cons these days, but really, all you need is a serviceable tent and a great location. Farrs puts the cherry on top with solar-powered hot showers hidden inside quirky converted horse boxes, compost loos and cattle troughs transformed into hand washing stations – but, otherwise, this campsite really is simplicity itself.

This is a tents-only campsite, so leave your campervan at home. Cars are also limited and are parked at the bottom of the site away from view, but a quad bike is on hand to help you transport all your kit to your pitch. Like your creature comforts? There's some of those on offer, too. The field is home to three traditional Kyrgyz yurts that make for a very cosy nomadic hideaway, especially if the weather isn't looking wonderful. Two handbuilt caravans inspired by Romani vardos and two shepherd's huts have a double bed and two camp beds each, plus wood burners, so they're great for sharing as a family – and for warming up in when the weather gets crisper as summer comes to a close.

> **Join your fellow campers and sit on the big logs arranged around a central campfire to swap stories at twilight, when the tiny bats and luminous glow worms that also live here come out to join the party**

Farrs is here for a good time, but not a long time – it's open from June until the nip of autumn weather rolls around in early October. In total, there are only 21 tent pitches and ten glamping options here, so there's a nice sense of space. You'll never feel like you're rubbing shoulders with the camping masses, festival-style. If you fancy roasting bangers for breakfast and marshmallows before bed, bring your own fire pit – the site has firewood for sale with an honesty box. Or join your fellow campers and sit on the big logs arranged around a central campfire to swap stories at twilight, when the tiny bats and luminous glow worms that also live here come out to join the party.

This is the ideal spot to practise the art of doing nothing much, but more active campers can start their day by following the footpath to reach the River Stour for a morning swim, or stroll across the fields to the pretty hamlet of Pamphill for lunch in the unique National Trust-owned Vine pub (the Trust looks after 30 historic inns), home to one of Britain's smallest bars and owned by the same family for an astonishing 150 years. Or bring your bike and explore National Cycle Network Route 25, which runs past the campsite and will lead you to Poole and the Dorset coast, a mere eight miles away. Or just, you know, chill out – this is the camping Good Life.

Wild *Escapes*

On the doorstep

Go fish: Fancy your hand at catching your own supper? Farr's can arrange fly and course fishing on the River Stour, so you can bake your very own brown trout over a fire pit come evening. Fishing permits are sold on-site for grown-ups (children under 13 don't need one).

Walk the Jurassic Coast: The glorious sweep of Lulworth Cove is a 40-minute drive away, and makes a great jumping-off point for walking and fossil-hunting along the Jurassic Coast to reach the iconic limestone sea arch of Durdle Door, five miles to the east.

A short walk from the campsite, you'll find Eye Bridge and River Stour, a perfect spot for wild swimming.

Wild *Escapes*

Old Smock Mill, Kent

Is there anything more romantic than holing up in a windmill? Old Smock Mill is missing its original wooden sails, and its cogs grind no more, but otherwise this beautiful building is untouched. Its four floors, clad in white weather board, are ideal for looking out over the lush, green Weald of Kent.

A 'smock mill', in case you're wondering, is a type of windmill with a sloping and usually shingled tower with either six or eight sides. The charming name comes from the fact that this design resembled the smocks once worn by Kentish farmers. The Old Smock Mill, first built in the 1800s, is a perfectly restored example, still with its original cogs and pulleys intact. It was a working mill until the Second World War, when it was taken over for a more military role – as a gunner's outlook – before finally being zhuzhed up into its current cosy, cottage-like state. If you've ever felt jealous of TV sleuth Jonathan Creek's eccentric windmill home, the carefully curated interior of the tower at Old Smock Mill will be right up your street.

Each hexagonally-shaped floor at the Old Smock Mill has its own name, and an oak staircase winds up to join each one. First is the honeycomb-shaped kitchen, known as the Meal Floor (as this was where ground wheat meal would originally be processed), with cupboards wrapped around one side and a big dining table to gather around, plus a sitting area with a leather sofa and a wood burner. You'll also find a clutch of organic eggs donated by the chickens next door, ready for a

The charming name comes from the fact that this design resembled the smocks once worn by Kentish farmers

sunny-side-up breakfast come morning. Doors from the Meal Floor lead out to the roomy oak 'staging' balcony, which completely encircles the mill, for panoramic views with your coffee or dinner in the open air at the round teak table. Downstairs, there's a small lawn shaded by an apple tree where you can grill a seaside-inspired feast (fresh Sussex scallops, perhaps) on the barbeque.

An oak staircase winds up to the Stone Floor, where massive millstones were once stored. The soaring ceiling appears propped up with a net of honey-coloured beams, under which is a huge double bed and a copper washing basin. A spiral staircase leads up further to the Dust Floor, still home to the mill's original winding mechanism, and now also to the bathroom, where pride of place is given to a deep, claw-footed bath.

The briny air of the Sussex coast is only a half-hour drive from Old Smock Mill – the nearest beach is Camber Sands which, unusually for East Sussex, has miles of yellow sand rather than pebbles, and is fringed by dunes. Close to the beach are the cobbled streets of the town of Rye, packed with antique shops, enticing cafés and cosy old pubs. Back at the mill, a footpath runs past the door and leads to the village green at old-fashioned Benenden. You might find you don't stray far from here, though – there's no need to tilt at windmills when you're staying at the perfect one instead.

Above (left to right): The main bedroom. The resident geese in the owner's garden.

Below: The living space on the first floor. The mill has been sympathetically renovated, while providing a modern, luxury interior for guests.

On the doorstep

Row the River Rother: Rent a rowing boat to drift along the glassily calm waters of the Rother, which was used to power local windmills as far back as 1086. Boats are available from Bodiam Boating Station or the Lime Wharf Café – the river's wild shores are best enjoyed with a picnic packed in the prow.

Bodiam Castle: 14th-century Bodiam Castle is straight out of an adventure from the age of chivalry, complete with moat, portcullis and ruined walls once guarded by knights. A 5½-mile/2-hour loop that crosses fields of hops and vines and visits the war memorial at Sandhurst Cross as well as the castle is reached via a 15-minute drive from Old Smock Mill.

Chapel House Farm Campsite, Herefordshire

The search for the simple life is over – it's secreted away in a wildflower meadow in the Welsh Marches.

Among Chapel House Farm Campsite's 6ha (15 acres), technically in England but within waving distance of the Welsh border, are three camping meadows that have just a handful of pitches mown into the grass, leaving most of the site as a haven for wildlife. The circular pitches are enormous, easily swallowing a campervan or a yurt, and the half-moon pitches are ideal for smaller tents. Even on the busiest summer weekend, there's tons of space at Chapel House, but the best time to visit is in early summer, when the tall grass encircling every tent is ablaze with wild flowers, including common spotted orchids, oxeye daisies and eyebright.

Picking your pitch is a pleasure – from the Flat Field, there is a view of far-off Hay Bluff and its surrounding hills; the Main Meadow has a sociable vibe, and the intimate Church Field has just two pitches, surrounded by ancient woodland.

When you've chosen your favourite pitch and set up camp, it's a steep stroll down the hill to the farmhouse, where you'll find all the campsite's useful bits and bobs – water taps, composting and rainwater loos and a covered space for washing dishes. The showers are rather fancy at Chapel House – they're slotted into an oak-framed hut with a chestnut shingle roof (inspired by Saxon-Romanian field barns), have cheery Mexican tiles on the walls and provide plenty of hot water from solar panels.

The best time to visit is in early summer, when the tall grass encircling every tent is ablaze with wild flowers, including common spotted orchids, oxeye daisies and eyebright

The farmhouse shop next door stocks homegrown produce, such as cuts of pork and lamb ready to put on the coals, home-cured charcuterie and bacon, garden herbs and locally-produced beer, cider and apple juice. If you like your food consciously reared and with as few miles attached to it as possible, this is definitely the place to shop for your supper. Each camping pitch comes with a fire pit and a tripod to get you sizzling your farm goodies on the flames.

Foodies who don't feel like cooking are also in for a treat. Make a beeline for Chapel House Farm on Friday nights, when a 15th-century oven is fired up and the owners make sourdough pizzas using home-grown flour and toppings (the nduja, new potato and rosemary pizza is pretty special). Mid-week feast nights are sometimes held in the old stable, which has a log fire and a roof to shelter under on chillier nights.

Kids roam free-range alongside the farm's unflappable chickens and are welcome to build dens in the 0.5ha (2 acres) of ancient woods, play games among the tall grass, or to go spying for some frequent visitors to the farm – red kites and buzzards soar overhead, and muntjac deer like to snuffle about in the meadows early in the morning.

For adventuring further afield, both the temptingly-named Black Mountains (their brooding title comes from the Saxons) and the dramatic peaks of the Brecon Beacons are easily reached by car from Chapel House Farm, so you can tramp the green hills before you return for a fire and a feast among the bluebells and the buttercups of these bucolic borderlands.

Wild *Escapes*

On the doorstep

Climb Hay Bluff: It's a short (if sharp) one-mile hike up to Hay Bluff's 677m (2,220ft) summit, which straddles the border of Wales and England. Alternatively, you can walk a 6-mile/2-hour loop to tackle Lord Hereford's Knob (no laughing, please, it's a mountain) for wonderful views over the Wye Valley. Hay Bluff is a 15-minute drive or 1¼-hour walk from the campsite.

Llanthony Priory: Ruins don't get more romantic than this former priory in the Vale of Ewyas, a 45-minutes drive or about two hours by bike from Chapel House, where Norman knight William de Lacy founded a hermitage in the 12th century. Nowadays, you can wander below its soaring walls and archways, open to the elements and with mountain peaks rising behind.

Top to bottom: One of the yurts available at the campsite. Inside Peter's Wagon, where you can switch off with a board game. The campsite's resident collie dog.

Lyveden Cottage, Northamptonshire

'It is remarkable how closely the history of the apple tree is connected with that of man,' wrote American naturalist Henry David Thoreau; he could easily have been thinking of the orchards at Lyveden, a National Trust estate in Northamptonshire. Once home to the Tresham family, this Elizabethan pile includes a manor house, a moated garden, a picturesque ruin and even a recently unearthed apple orchard, now restored to its original splendour. It's a charmingly romantic place to explore – especially after hours, when you'll get all of its wildness to yourself.

The home of a former forester, Lyveden Cottage sits among the wildflower meadows above the manor house, with its own snug garden hidden from view. On the ground floor, there's a kitchen overlooking the herb garden, a rather grand dining room with a large inglenook fireplace and homely sitting room with a wood burner (a very cosy spot to hole up in on rainy days). Upstairs you'll find three bedrooms (two doubles and one single) all overlooking the garden. Big iron bedsteads draped in blankets are the perfect place to wake up to peace and quiet – well, except for the rather chirpy birds, that love to visit the front garden at breakfast time and will thank you for crumpet crumbs.

What's so special about this postcard-worthy cottage is that once evening rolls around and Lyveden closes for the day, you can explore the estate in perfect solitude. Wander around the wildflower-lined moat, now partly restored to its former glory, and the apple orchard, where in spring pink blossoms bloom and in autumn fat Winter Queening apples (the very same variety that were planted here in Elizabethan times) hang heavy from the boughs. Try to tread quietly while you go, though – you're likely to spot local wildlife, including grazing rabbits, red kites circling overhead and even curious little muntjac deer, who like to come out to forage during the more peaceful times of day.

The cottage's own small garden, hidden by hedges and lavender bushes, is a sunny spot for tea and toast under the tall cherry tree. A wooden gate leads you out into a meadow that's ablaze with yellow cowslips (the county flower of Northamptonshire) and primroses in spring, as well as violets, bluebells and cuckooflowers. It's also here that you'll find one of the strangest secrets of Lyveden. A stone's throw from the cottage is the grand and rather curious ruin of Lyveden New Bield.

Ruins don't come more picturesque than this abandoned folly. It looks as if it's been left to crumble, but in fact Lyveden New Bield was never finished, and stands open to the elements just as the stonemasons left it back in 1605. Sir Thomas Tresham, for whom the lodge, the orchard and the gardens were created, lived at Lyveden Old Bield and died before his 'garden lodge' was finished. It was a turbulent time in Britain. Tresham was persecuted for his Catholic faith by Elizabeth I, and his descendants didn't fare much better – Sir Thomas' son Francis was part of the Gunpowder Plot's failed attempt to blow up King James I's parliament. The gardens fell into disrepair, but by 2013, Lyveden was being cared for by the National Trust, who have worked to restore this magical landscape, planting apple trees and maintaining the moated gardens exactly as Thomas Tresham wished. Now you can stay and wander around this tantalising link with the past, ever-unfinished and frozen in time.

> **A charmingly romantic place to explore – especially after hours, when you'll get all of its wildness to yourself**

*Below (left to right): Explore the orchard after hours.
The garden at Lyveden Cottage is full of herbs and
flowers in spring.*

*Opposite: Lyveden Cottage sits next to the ruins of
Lyveden New Bield, surrounded by meadows and fields.*

Wild *Escapes*

On the doorstep

Walk the Lyveden Way: This 10-mile/2–3-hour hiking route is the perfect sampler of Northamptonshire, taking in woodland, open countryside and pretty villages as well as cutting right past Lyveden New Bield itself. The walk is circular, so you can be back in time for tea in the cottage.

Potter around Oundle: The pleasant market town of Oundle, 4½ miles/1½ hours from Lyveden on foot, is a mix of old-world cottages and foodie cafés. The Falcon Inn makes a great mid-hike pitstop.

Wild *Escapes*

Opposite: Hallway leading to the dining room.
Left: Curl up in the cosy living room.
Above: The master bedroom.
Below: The secluded garden at the front of the cottage.

Blacksmith's Cottage, Norfolk

You might just mistake Blacksmith's Cottage for a gingerbread house from a distance – this pocket-sized cottage of ruddy red bricks, with a traditional thatched roof of local Norfolk reed popped on top, looks straight out of a children's story at first glance.

But what's extra special about Blacksmith's is where it is – secreted away in a corner of Norfolk's beautiful Blickling Estate. A grand Jacobean house, dainty formal gardens and an astonishing 1,860ha (4,600 acres) of meadows, parkland and woodland are your extended back garden when you stay here. And when other visitors head home at the end of each day, it's just you and a handful of other holiday guests that are free to roam all over.

Whatever your outdoorsy itch, you're likely to find it tended to at Blickling. Green-fingered visitors will love the restored gardens, from the elegant orangery and the parterre, an intricate Victorian design of yew hedges and roses, to the walled kitchen garden, stocked with herbs and home-grown produce. Hikers can dip a booted toe in the estate's huge swathe of land. The Acre, a sweep of grassy meadow crowned by a turkey oak, makes for a beautiful short walk, while wildlife watchers will want to head into the woods, home to woodpeckers, barn owls and deer, or stand still on the edge of the lake in the morning, where water birds dip below a cloak of mist.

If two wheels are more your bag, there is a store for bikes at the cottage so you can stash your wheels ready to hit

Wildlife watchers will want to head into the woods, home to woodpeckers, barn owls and deer, or stand still on the edge of the lake in the morning, where water birds dip below a cloak of mist

the trail, and the cycle hub at Blickling also rents out bikes and provides maps of the estate trails. There are even live gigs to entice music lovers – in July and August each year Blickling hosts open-air concerts, and the warm summer air is filled with melodies of an evening.

History buffs will be happy, too. Blickling has its fair share of weird and wonderful mysteries, including two secret tunnels to seek out in the grounds; but the most impressive is the 200-year-old Mausoleum, an eerie stone pyramid where the remains of John Hobart, 2nd Earl of Buckinghamshire, and his two wives are buried. Traces of another famous resident have all but vanished from the landscape at Blickling; it was once the site of the medieval manor house where Queen of England, Anne Boleyn, was born in around 1501. Well, almost all trace – the story goes that each year on 17 May, the anniversary of Anne's execution at the hands of her fickle husband, Henry VIII, her headless ghost roams the grounds.

When you've had your fill of apparitions of the past, head home to the decidedly less haunted Blacksmith's Cottage. It is warm and welcoming under the thatch, and beautiful old wooden beams criss-cross the ceilings of the sitting room, which hasn't changed much since its time as an estate worker's cottage. The roomy kitchen is the perfect spot to whip up a cake in time for tea and upstairs are two bedrooms, one double and one twin, decorated in cool pastel hues. Outside, a large, enclosed lawn is perfect for picnics, or just for basking in the sunshine and feeling to the manor born.

Top: Blickling cottage looks like a gingerbread house from a distance.

Left: The sunlight shines into the living room.

Opposite: A short walk from the cottage is Blickling estate parkland, stunning to explore in the early morning.

Wild *Escapes*

On the doorstep

Swim on the coast: The Norfolk coast is a 20-minute drive from Blacksmith's Cottage – Cromer Beach's sand-and-shingle shore is a great spot for a dip. The seaside town is also famous for its locally-caught crabs – pick up a few to take back to the cottage for supper.

Go seal spotting: Blakeney National Nature Reserve's salt marshes are 20 miles from the cottage and are home to the UK's largest grey seal colony, along with their friends the little terns, which nest here. Walk the four miles of shingle spit at low tide to reach the sand dunes and keep an eye out for newborn seal pups in autumn and winter. To see the seals up close, join a boat trip from Morston Quay.

Rockhouse Retreat, Worcestershire

Ready to rock out? Deep in a wall of rich red sandstone in Worcestershire's Habberley Valley is a home where you can get in touch with your inner troglodyte and see what it feels like to be a cave dweller for a few days. The Rockhouse has been inhabited for the past 800 years, but was left a ruin before being lovingly restored into a hidden hideaway that's big on Palaeolithic charm.

The cliffs that surround the retreat are an astonishing 250 million years old and are said to have inspired J. R. R. Tolkien when he dreamed up *The Hobbit*. They look out over 1.2 hectares (3 acres) of private woodland, home to hooting owls and a babbling brook. The red rock doesn't give much sign of the house tucked away inside – it's been left as natural as possible, with oak windows cut into its face giving a clue to the wonders awaiting within.

Outside there's a terrace where you can sit in the shade thrown by the rocks on a sunny day, looking out on a view unchanged by the millennia. Inside, however, this unique bolthole is nothing like the Stone Age – instead, it's the epitome of cosy, with whitewashed walls and a cottagey feel. Lamps and windows in the wall that faces the trees mean it doesn't feel gloomy, and the floor is cleverly designed to ventilate the house in summer and heat it in winter. There's a wood-burning stove to stuff with logs for a comforting crackle as you read a book or cook up a stew on the Aga. The bathroom, with a mosaic of pebbles pressed into the shower and a sink made of fossilised wood, feels like you're washing in a grotto, and the bedroom, inspired by the cave houses

This is a journey to Middle Earth by way of the Black Country

of Italy, is the perfect place to tuck yourself away in the total quiet of ancient stone walls. This is a journey to Middle Earth by way of the Black Country.

If you are ready to roll away the stone and go exploring you can delve into the history of cave dwellings at Kinver Edge that are very similar to your Hobbit hole. Here, the National Trust care for a cluster of rock houses that were once homes for farm labourers and gamekeepers, right up until the 1960s. Several are now restored to show visitors how they were lived in through the centuries – some are simple caves still carved with age-old graffiti; others are snug candlelit cottages recreated with the help of photos and with working fires where you may catch a volunteer making toast.

There are still some permanent residents of this hidden spot once known as the 'Switzerland of the Midlands' – lesser horseshoe bats like to flit about at dusk. There's also a National Trust café where they serve – you guessed it – rock cakes to go with your cuppa. You can work them off with a wander in the wildlife-rich heathland of Kinver Edge, crowned with an Iron Age hillfort with far-reaching views to the Cotswolds and the Malvern hills. Just as fascinating are the old orchards and vegetable patches still tended here, and which once fed the last of Britain's cave-dwellers.

Wild *Escapes*

On the doorstep

Walk the River Severn: Running close by the Rockhouse, the Severn Way follows the course of the River Severn south to reach the cover of Wyre Forest (5 miles/1 hour 40 minutes). A serious hike to the north (12½ miles/4¼ hours) takes you to the hamlet of Eardington. From here, you can watch the Severn Valley Railway's trains puff along, or continue along to Bridgenorth station to catch a steam-powered ride.

Wander in Wyre Forest: Walk among 26 sq. km (10 sq. miles) of ancient oaks and statuesque fir trees in some of the oldest woodland in Britain at Wyre, to which the Rockhouse sits adjacent. Hiking, cycling and horse-riding trails criss-cross the forest, and you can rent bikes as well as a tramper (an off-road mobility vehicle) to go further afield.

Top and left: Get cosy inside the Rockhouse, with pre-historic inspired details everywhere, including a modern cave-painting on the wall.

Right: Cook up a feast on the fire pit outside, while surrounded by peaceful woodland.

On the Water

The wonders of wild swimming

Human beings are 60 per cent water, so perhaps it is no surprise that swimming outdoors can feel like coming home. Immersing yourself in an empty lake or the rolling ocean frees your mind, stretches out your limbs and washes away the stresses of the modern world.

Wild swimming has become something of a collective obsession in Britain over the past decade, as more and more of us discover what science has proved to be true – that cold-water swimming lowers stress levels, acts as a natural painkiller and can even alleviate anxiety and depression. A dip outdoors can take you to some of the most beautiful corners of the country, from aquamarine-coloured Welsh tidal pools to deep Cornish quarries reclaimed by nature; from glittering Scottish rivers hidden deep in the woods to peaceful oases in the heart of our biggest cities. Some swim spots have seen generations of bathing Britons come and go – at the Hampstead Heath Ponds in the heart of the capital, Londoners have been taking to the cool green waters since the 1860s. Apart from the occasional plane leaving white, fluffy contrails in the sky overhead, nothing has really changed.

It's easy to forget about the joys of wild swimming come winter. When daylight hours are precious and it is bitterly cold outside, we naturally want to hibernate indoors and shy away from the idea of dipping our toes into freezing water. But if you're brave and take a leaf out of the book of Scandinavian swimmers, you might find that cold weather swimming is an amazing coping mechanism for fighting off the winter doldrums. Finnish and Swedish swimmers have known about the mental and physical benefits of cold-water immersion for centuries – talviuinti (the ritual of a swim in icy – or even ice-clad – lakes) is well-known for its health benefits, proven to stimulate circulation and boost mood. It might well be the reason that the Finns are officially the happiest nation on the planet. And now outdoor swim clubs and solo dippers all over Britain get in the water year-round in pursuit of happiness too, with lidos open throughout the winter, hardy Scottish swimmers breaking ice off the surface of lochs of a morning and New Year's Day sea swims becoming an annual ritual across the country.

It's important to stay safe when outdoor swimming. Much of this is common sense – don't swim after alcohol, swim with a buddy and pay attention to your surroundings. Don't jump into a river or lake without knowing the depth of the water first; have a plan for getting out safely, and check if there are currents or rip tides in the ocean, or a fast-flowing current in a river, before you take the plunge. Be aware that, in winter, your stamina can be cut shorter by the cold – wear a warm wetsuit, and consider a brightly coloured swim cap and swimming buoy, so you're easy to spot in the water. Never swim in stagnant water, in reservoirs or anywhere with 'No Swimming' signs – even if the water looks tempting, it's usually prohibited because it's either dangerous or could affect a fragile, protected environment.

A dip outdoors can take you to some of the most beautiful corners of the country

When you do swim, you'll be in good company – 7.5 million people in Britain now describe themselves as open water swimmers. And don't forget any new friends below the surface. The UK may not be the first place you'd pick as a snorkelling hotspot, but the clear waters off Wales and Scotland, and even some in south-west England, are fantastic places to go on an underwater safari to meet our incredible indigenous wildlife. You can spot scuttling crabs in Pembrokeshire, rare seahorses in Dorset, flat sunfish off Sark in the Channel Islands, and even swim with basking sharks and porpoises in Scotland. Or go south for one of the most rewarding winter wildlife encounters in Britain – snorkelling with a colony of friendly and curious seals. Head to St Martin's, a tiny, car-free island that's part of the subtropical Isles of Scilly archipelago off the coast of Cornwall, to jump into the water with these puppyish characters, who like to come up to say hello and have even been known to gently nibble on snorkellers' flippers.

Wherever you choose to dip, with just one swim you'll instantly feel connected to the natural world. Try wild swimming regularly, and you'll start to notice how ever-changing our blue planet is, as spring wild flowers bloom on river banks, summer warms the surface of sunny sea coves, autumn scatters pools with golden leaves and winter turns down the temperature of lakes to toe-curling but exhilarating levels of cold. Perhaps it's time to step away from the bustle of the air above the surface, just for a moment, and explore another element.

Above: Wild swimming in the Peak District.
Left: Riverside fauna.

Wild *Escapes*

The Riverside, Surrey

'Picture yourself on a boat on a river, with tangerine trees and marmalade skies': live out The Beatles' dreamy 'Lucy in the Sky' lyrics at The Riverside, a cabin right on the waters of the River Wey where sunsets turn the water shades of apricot, and you can drift along in your own rowing boat.

The Riverside has always been a haven – this Arcadian wooden cabin was built in the 1930s as an escape for smog-addled city types from London. It's hard to believe the capital is just 25 miles away from this peaceful place, where very little happens besides the odd swan floating by, even though you're actually on a small tributary of the busy River Thames. The tranquil Wey was one of the first British rivers to be made navigable, and opened to barge traffic in 1653. Today, it's the only canal looked after by the National Trust, and it's one with a mystery – Papercourt Lock, right by Riverside, was built in 1766 and moved in the 1780s, but no-one knows why.

These days, the cabin on its banks is a pleasing mishmash of eye-catching pieces, from Arts & Crafts stained glass to 70s furniture. Inside is compact and will please lovers of the tiny house movement – the main living space is arranged around a wood burner backed by tiles, and leads on to the double bedroom, where you can lie in white sheets and watch the ducks outside. The cabin is simple – power comes from the sun and there's no TV or Wi-Fi connection (swap them for books and board games instead), but the modest wood-clad kitchen area does have all the kit you need for a cracking feast. You can squeeze in more

A cabin right on the waters of the River Wey where sunsets turn the water shades of apricot, and you can drift along in your own rowing boat

water babies if you need to – there's a spare single bunk up on a platform, and the vintage sofa doubles up as a fold-out bed.

The wonderful sense of space at Riverside comes from its huge windows, which open out fully onto the decking and the river. Outside, two duck egg-blue Adirondack chairs keep watch over the bucolic view, and there's a round wooden table and a fire pit on the riverbank for a lazy lunch.

Your very own white wooden rowing boat is moored on the decking, ready to set sail up the river and there's also an inflatable kayak to paddle about in, or you can go for full immersion by diving among the reeds for a swim in the river's cool green water, where steel-blue dragonflies flit at eye level. When night falls, the river is the domain of a new set of visitors – listen for the hoot of owls and watch the inky skies for the fluttering wings of bats as you stoke the flames of the fire pit and watch their golden reflection in the dark water.

The only big decision to make each morning at The Riverside is where to wander to for lunch. Even the local pubs have names straight out of a storybook – sit in the suntrap garden at The Jovial Sailor, have supper at The Clock House or head to The Half Moon on a Sunday – it does a slap-up roast. Best of all, you can row, row, row your boat along the Wey straight from the cabin to reach The Anchor pub, and moor up for a sundowner. Take it slow – in the words of writer A. A. Milne, 'rivers know this: there is no hurry. We shall get there some day.'

On the doorstep

RHS Wisley: One of the world's most revered gardens, RHS Wisley, a 13-minute drive from The Riverside, is a riot of flowers in spring and summer, and a wonderful spot for leaf peeping in autumn, when the trees turn gold and 1,000 species of heather put on a rich purple display. From here it is a short walk onto Wisley Common, over 300ha (800 acres) of woodland, rare heathland and wetland.

Dapdune Wharf: The award-winning visitor centre at Dapdune Wharf in Guildford, a 15-minute drive or a 2½-hour walk away, tells the story of the navigations and the people who lived and worked on them. Visitors can see where the huge Wey barges were built and climb aboard Reliance, one of three surviving barges.

Below: Glass doors looking out from the cabin onto the river.

Opposite (left to right, top to bottom): The cabin is filled with carefully-selected antique furnishings. Explore the river on your own rowing boat. The surrounding Papercourt Lock and Weir is cared for by the National Trust. Get warm around the fire pit in the garden adjoining the river.

Ditchling Cabin, East Sussex

Pack your swimsuit and escape to a secluded cabin on the water's edge. Ditchling Cabin, set on its very own lake in the South Downs National Park in Sussex, is the perfect place to hole up in if you're a fan of the life aquatic – you can dive straight in from the wraparound wooden deck, where a fleet of different water craft are tied up waiting for adventure.

While this A-frame cabin doesn't actually float on the surface of its private 1-ha (2½-acre) fishing lake, it feels like it does, with wooden decking leading straight to the water and no less than three wooden pontoons that you can dive off or sunbathe on surrounding the cabin. A rowing boat, a raft and a clutch of canoes and kayaks are moored up, and they and the lake are all yours for your stay.

Dive straight in from the cabin's wraparound wooden deck, where a fleet of different water craft are tied up waiting for adventure

Indeed, life on deck is very easy at Ditchling Cabin, which comes equipped with everything you need to spend time in the sunshine, including a barbeque, fire pit (plus a ready supply of marshmallows) and a closet full of wetsuits to borrow. There's also – joy of joys for keen swimmers – a hot outdoor shower to warm up under and a hot tub to soak in after a dip, and even an outdoor wine fridge for oenophiles.

A stay at this dreamy cabin may be all about splashing about in the great outdoors, but once you retreat inside, you'll find a cosy main living space complete with wood burner, squashy sofa and plenty of books and board games for entertainment, plus a kitchen area with a big dining table. Downstairs there's also a minute loo – the shower has to be braved outside but

does have plenty of hot water. The interior is a curated delight of American-backwoods cabin meets old-school Scouting hut meets fisherman chic, complete with nets and rods lining the walls and a chess set laid out by the fire. The windows frame trees and glassy water (and nothing else), and the sitting room doors fold back so you can eat outside on the decking – pick wild garlic in the nearby woods in spring or catch your own fish to barbeque outdoors in the summer.

Climb the stairs to the top floor to find the enormous bedroom. Pride of place is a roll-top metal bath by the window, for a view of the lake as you wash. You're guaranteed a good night's sleep in the huge white double bed, and downstairs two dinky single beds are hidden away in a wooden cupboard – a lovely hidey-hole for children. If there are a few more of you, you can also pitch a tent in the garden to squeeze everyone in.

Ditchling feels very secluded – it's just you and the lake here, but you're bang in the South Downs National Park, Britain's newest National Park and home to rolling hills of chalk and grasslands, rare healthland, dark skies perfect for stargazing and wild trails for hiking and trail running. Hilly roads lead down to the sea for cycling, and the Green Welly Café in Ditchling village has a pretty walled garden to pop to for lunch. But really, it's hard to find the motivation to roam far from the cabin when you could just crack open a beer and sit in a low-slung Adirondack chair or a bobbing row boat and watch the sun set low over your very own lake.

On the doorstep

Stomp along the South Downs Way: A short ramble or, if you're feeling energetic, a five-minute trail run will take you from the cabin and onto the 100-mile South Downs Way, where you can walk along a winding ridge of chalky grassland that looks out over Sussex.

Cycle to the sea: Bring your bike – it's an hour's road cycle from the cabin to reach Brighton's seafront. Along the way be sure to climb the 248-m (813-ft) Ditchling Beacon, its panoramic views are a must. In medieval times the summit was the site of a warning beacon that was kept ready to light in the event of an imminent invasion.

Wild *Escapes*

Opposite: Stylish interiors in the living area at Ditchling Cabin.
Below: The deck of the cabin includes a hot tub, outdoor dining area, BBQ, deck chairs and your choice of three boats.

Ditchling cabin at dusk.

Opposite (left to right): Views from Ditchling Beacon nearby. Relax in a roll top bathtub in the upstairs bedroom, with views of the private lake.

Wild *Escapes*

The Raft at Chigborough, Essex

A fantasy of the American Wild West that looks like it's crash-landed in a peaceful Essex backwater, The Raft at Chigborough is just that – a wide wooden platform with a two-storey cabin perched on top, tethered to the bottom of a reed-lined lake. To reach it, you can either stash your bags on board a small boat and row yourself across, or use the floating ferry platform to cross the water. Then it's just you, the cabin and the lake – hidden away in your own little moated hideaway.

Come aboard this solar-powered cabin, made of hand-sawed pine logs, for a quick tour. The sun-dappled living space is furnished with a bright rug, big sofa-bed, wood-burner and solar-powered lights. Wooden shelves hold all the accessories you need for the simple life – games, plenty of books, a wind-up radio and vintage telescope for stargazing. Glass doors open onto the decking and bring the sounds of nature in on sultry days. The bedroom is a lofty mezzanine, with a double bed tucked under a skylight, so you can watch the stars blink one by one before bed. There's also an upstairs balcony with soaring views of the water and surrounding woodland.

The pioneer-style kitchen is outdoors and comes complete with gas hobs, a fridge and a hefty barbeque.

The sun sets slowly at The Raft – and the best place to watch it is from your very own wood-fired hot tub, perched on the main bank of the lake

You'll definitely end up spending most of your time cooking outside or just soaking in the surroundings – chairs face the lake for a morning cuppa and there's a hammock swaying from two wooden posts, perfect for an afternoon nap. Even the shower is outside, for a wash with a view.

This is, naturally, a wonderful place for spotting aquatic wildlife, from the gaggle of swans that like to visit the Raft, to peacock-blue kingfishers glimpsed in the trees, or the splash of trout in the depths (you can also fish one out for your supper). Binoculars on board will help identify what you spot. You can't swim in the lake, but if the jumping trout make the water look tempting, the Essex coast is only a few minutes' walk away from the cabin for a dip, and bikes are also provided for exploring further afield.

The sun sets slowly at The Raft – and the best place to watch it is from your very own wood-fired hot tub, perched on the main bank of the lake. Row yourself across with a bottle or two for an unobstructed view. There's a fire pit with a collection of logs stashed away, so you can warm up around the flames before you row home again. To find your inner Huckleberry Finn, the only way, it seems, is Essex.

On the doorstep

Stroll along the coast: Walk to the coast path from the cabin and turn left to reach Heybridge Basin (one mile) to watch boats bob in the harbour. Stop for lunch in the popular seafood shack, then continue along for another four miles to reach Northey Island, a nature reserve cared for by the National Trust, known as the wildest place in Essex. Book ahead if you want to explore further – Northey is reached by crossing a causeway at low tide.

Go fishing: Trout and coarse fishery are both available at Chigborough – you can fish to your heart's content right from the cabin's decking if you fancy catching your own lunch, and lessons on the lake for netting newbies are also available.

Boats at Heybridge Basin.
Above: A hammock on the deck of the floating cabin.
Right: BBQ on the deck of the cabin.

The Raft floating cabin, viewed from the rowing boat which you can take out onto the private lake.

The Boy John, Aberdyfi, Gwynedd

Set sail for a night or two aboard The Boy John – it may not leave dry land, but this beached boat, run aground on the shores of the Dyfi Valley estuary in mid-Wales, makes a magical stay for sea lovers.

Even the address of this former fishing trawler – The Boy John, Smuggler's Cove, Frongoch Boatyard – sounds temptingly romantic. And 'John' lives up to expectations. This rustic wreck is definitely not a grand stay, but it's a comfy – and decidedly quirky – one.

Inside this wood-lined boat, you'll find sofas arranged around a wood burner and shelves stacked with nature books – plus a breakfast table at port side and even an upright piano at starboard, in case you fancy starting up some sea shanties of an evening. A small kitchen area in the bow of the boat is all skew-whiff angles and sloping ceilings hung with bunting, but this little space squeezes in two gas rings to cook up a seafood feast on, as well as a fridge and a sink. Head downstairs and into the stern to find the double bedroom, where portholes look westward towards the Ynyslas sand dunes – and towards the setting sun, which paints the sands red and gold on clear days. The bench in the sitting area upstairs also converts into a basic double bed for children, if they don't mind the sleeping arrangements (dogs are allowed onboard as extra stowaways). Guests need to bring their own bedding, but a wheelbarrow is provided to help you lug your creature comforts to the boat. Less romantic but important – a shower and a toilet are steps away in the boatyard and are shared with the small Smuggler's Cove's campsite.

> **Portholes look westward towards the Ynyslas sand dunes – and towards the setting sun, which paints the sands red and gold on clear days**

Bring your binoculars, as the boat makes a fabulous place to keep an eye on the estuary, especially for wildlife enthusiasts. The downstairs cabin has a big corner window with truly breathtaking views of the Dyfi Estuary, including across to Ynys-hir RSPB nature reserve and the towering peaks of Snowdonia National Park in the distance. Keep your eyes peeled for the ospreys and otters who visit in the summer, migrating waders in autumn and, if you're really lucky, the Greenland white-fronted goose in winter – this is its only territory in England and Wales. The guidebooks aboard will help identify what you spot. Don't stop watching at night – on clear nights you can see the Milky Way arching over the boat.

Hop off deck and you're in a boatyard and campsite known as Smuggler's Cove. This is a working boatyard, near a road and railway line, so it's not a remote retreat. That said, you don't need to go far to feel immersed in the seascape – soak up the sights from the seating area right outside The Boy John, where there's a barbeque area and an open fire pit, lined with stones from the beach. Further afield, amateur scientists can roam the Dyfi UNESCO Biosphere Zone, which incorporates some of the most outstanding natural habitats in Europe – Ynyslas sand dunes and Borth bog to the south are both protected habitats in a Site of Special Scientific Interest.

On the doorstep

Dyfi's dunes: Keen biologists can explore the Dyfi National Nature Reserve from Ynyslas sand dunes, across the water from The Boy John. The estuary is home to internationally important mudflats, sandbanks and salt marsh, which provide feeding and roosting areas for wetland birds, and there are two easy 2-mile/45-minute walks mapped out at the visitor centre to help you explore.

Centre for Alternative Technology: Learn about practical solutions to help create a zero-carbon world at this lovingly constructed eco centre, reached by funicular and home to flower-packed greenhouses and a cosy café as well as working examples of the alternative technologies and green buildings of the future.

Opposite (left to right): Cooking on the outdoor fire pit on the shore of the estuary. Nautical details inside the boat. The boatyard is full of objects offering secrets to the history of The Boy John.

Below: On a clear night, the expansive skies are filled with stars.

Rose Castle Cottage, Cumbria

An Englishman's home is his castle, they say – and perhaps that's what architects had in mind when this small but surprisingly grand stone cottage was built back in the 19th century, situated in what must be one of the finest spots in the Lake District.

Once a local quarryman's home, Rose Castle Cottage is now a pleasingly simple holiday hideaway. A steep and narrow private track leads up to it; low-slung cars may complain a bit – it's a tough drive in summer and impassable in winter snows – but well worth the humps and bumps to leave tarmac and tourists behind and reach this eyrie, high above the glassy waters of Tarn Hows.

The cottage's original Victorian front door leads straight into the sitting room, and has a lovely secret tucked into the eaves – a swallow's nest where, in spring, you'll spot hungry nestlings making a racket while their patient parents are out hunting for food. The sitting room itself is kitted out with comfortable high-backed chairs and a sofa arranged around the cavernous old fireplace, where there's now a wood burner in pride of place.

Get the fire going as soon as you arrive – it heats the entire house, so it'll need a lot of feeding with logs from the cottage's store in cooler weather. If you're still mastering the art of fire building, there's also an immersion heater for a warm shower. A galley kitchen and a bathroom complete the downstairs. If you step out of the sitting room (and under the swallow's nest), there's a small dry-stone-walled garden with a big picnic table (just watch you keep the gate closed – the local Herdwick sheep and their inquisitive lambs love to join in). Upstairs are two bedrooms, one double and one twin, both with windows tucked under the cottage's crow-stepped gables looking out onto the surrounding hillsides speckled with grazing sheep.

Rose Castle is pretty free of modern technology – there's no TV or Wi-Fi connection, and the gentle interior doesn't feel that unchanged from its Victorian origins. Don't stay indoors for long, though – the great outdoors is calling.

A public footpath runs right past the cottage door from Tarn Hows and continues to the tip of Coniston Water, where you can catch a ride on the splendid heirloom of the steam yacht *Gondola*. For a gentler stroll, explore the landscape of Tarn Hows just below the cottage. If this limpid lake, lined with trees and with picturesque islands dotted on its surface, looks a little too beautiful to be natural, that's because it is – it is actually artificial, designed in the 1860s by industrialist James Garth Marshall as an ornamental masterpiece. You can't swim in tempting Tarn Hows – the lake is now a Site of Special Scientific Interest thanks to the wildlife it encourages. Instead, walk its shores and watch for tiny tree pipits in branches and leggy herons in the shallows, as well as the rare Belted Galloway cows that graze the lake's grassy edges.

> **A lovely secret tucked into the eaves – a swallow's nest where, in spring, you'll spot hungry nestlings making a racket while their patient parents are out hunting for food**

Above: Tarn Hows, a short walk from the cottage.

Left: Cosy up in the living room after a day of exploring the Lakes.

Opposite (top to bottom): A swallow rests on the picnic table in the garden. The cottage nestled in the Cumbrian landscape.

On the doorstep

Circular walk around Tarn Hows: A gentle and accessible 2-mile/1-hour ramble along the flattish wide path encircling the lake rewards with glorious views of the surrounding mountains and the lily pad-strewn waters. Wheelchair and pushchair-friendly.

Steam Yacht *Gondola* on Coniston Water: For a taste of Venice in the Lakelands, follow the footpath south 1¾ miles/40 minutes from the cottage down to Monk Coniston jetty, to catch the elegant steam-powered Steam Yacht *Gondola* for a nostalgic cruise on Coniston Water. This unique Victorian yacht, which slices through the water with a golden serpent as its figurehead, was lovingly rebuilt to its former glory in the 1970s by the National Trust.

Low Wray Campsite, Cumbria

Pitch a tent with glorious views of the Lake District's wild side at Low Wray, where you can paddle in the water by day and sleep under the stars (or even high up in the trees) at night. This shoreside site has everything that only the very best camping trips are made of.

Low Wray is right on the edge of Windermere, the ribbon of deep water that cuts through the heart of the South Lakes. Windermere, which gets its name from the old Norse, Vinandr mere (which just means 'Vinandr's lake') is one of the most popular lakes in Cumbria. At 10 miles long and a mile wide, it's also the largest, so there's always room to find some breathing space. In fact, the sense of space is in abundance here – the campsite has direct access to the lake for launching boats, as well as its own little beach where wild swimmers can enter the water and younger bathing fans can splash about safely.

Whatever kind of idyllic camping spot you're dreaming of, you're likely to find your perfect pitch at this sprawling campsite, with a choice of waterfront, lake, meadow and woodland settings. Pitches are well spaced, so you never feel like you're cheek-by-jowl with other campers, and if you fancy something a little more exciting than bringing your trusty old tent, the campsite has compact camping pods and capacious safari tents. You can also bring along your campervan. All the different mini environments are linked by meandering paths and footbridges, and cars are tucked well out of the way. Camping chores are made easier by Low Wray's handy facilities, too – on site are toilet and shower blocks, drying rooms washing-up areas and a shop well-stocked with games, toys, maps and groceries.

The most thrilling way to spend the night at Low Wray is by renting one of campsite's two quirky tree tents. These spherical canvas nests hang suspended in the trees and look rather like the homes of weaver birds. They are reached via a ladder, and a flap door leads into a surprisingly spacious cocoon that sleeps three. There's even a wood burner inside your new nest. On warm evenings you can lie and watch the stars come out through the sky window, and listen out for some fellow creatures – kingfishers, badgers, deer and otters are all regular visitors to Low Wray.

Walking paths wind away from the campsite towards Wray Castle along the shoreline or inland to Ambleside, and it's no problem if you haven't got your own adventure kit with you – the campsite has a colourful array of bikes, kayaks and paddleboards lined up by the shore available for campers to rent, and a permit isn't needed to paddle about on Windermere. Grab an oar and hit the water from the campsite's own calm bay, or head out into the web of biking trails within pedalling distance.

What time is it? S'mores o'clock. Open campfires aren't permitted at the campsite, but barbeques and fire pits definitely are, so you can still sizzle your sausages and roast a marshmallow or two in proper camping fashion once you're back from a jam-packed day of messing about on the water.

> **On warm evenings you can lie and watch the stars come out through the sky window, and listen out for some fellow creatures – kingfishers, badgers, deer and otters are all regular visitors**

On the doorstep

Climb Orrest Head: Alfred Wainwright wrote of this much-admired viewpoint: 'Orrest Head for many of us, is "where we came in" – our first ascent in Lakeland, our first sight of mountains in tumultuous array across glittering waters, our awakening to beauty. It is a popular walk, deservedly, for here the promised land is seen in all its glory.' All that's left to add to the famous guidebook writer's description is that there's an easy 3-mile/1¼-hour walking loop to Orrest for views across to the Lake District Fells, Morecambe Bay and the Pennines.

Kayak to an island: For a proper adventure, grab a kayak and go exploring to one of Windermere's 18 islands. Silver Holme was the inspiration for Cormorant Island in Arthur Ransome's *Swallows and Amazons*, or paddle across to The Lilies to admire this secluded spot's wild flowers in spring.

Opposite (top to bottom): Kitchen and seating area in the tree tents. Pitch up on the lakeside.
Above: Views of Lake Windermere.
Below: Paddleboarders on the lake in summer.

Wild *Escapes*

The Boathouse at Knotts End, Cumbria

The Taj Mahal. Machu Picchu. Easter Island. The Great Barrier Reef. The Grand Canyon. What these wonders of Planet Earth have in common is a UNESCO World Heritage status – and in 2017, England's Lake District joined their ranks, chosen for its spectacular and well cared-for landscape of soaring mountains interspaced with ribbons of glacial lakes.

Arguably the most peaceful spot from which to enjoy this lauded landscape is right on the shores of one of its finest lakes. At The Boathouse at Knotts End, you can practically reach out and touch the western shore of Ullswater.

First built as a working boathouse in the 19th century, the upper storage space at Knotts End is now an intimate cottage that's a riot of colour, antiques and quirky finds. Small is beautiful at The Boathouse – the sitting room doubles up as the bedroom, with a leather sofa tucked under white-painted beams leading through a wide archway to a king-size bed, where French windows fill the space with views of the lake and of far-off hills.

Light the wood burner before bed on chilly winter nights and you can have the simple pleasure of falling asleep to the warming glow of a fire. A small kitchen has enough gadgets that even the most dedicated foodie could need to whip up a Cumbrian feast of local ingredients. In the sitting room there's a small dining table for two, and beyond the bedroom a wooden Juliet balcony jutting out from the boathouse is a wonderful spot for lunch while you watch

Sit out and watch the sunset – and keep a weather eye out for the elusive otters who occasionally pop by at dusk or dawn

steamers and sailing boats glide past. There's plenty of privacy here – the boathouse is reached down a private track and is set in 4ha (10 acres) of private woodland. Underneath your little top-floor eyrie flow the waters of the lake, providing a calming soundtrack to life at Knotts End. Sit out and watch the sunset – and keep a weather eye out for the elusive otters who occasionally pop by at dusk or dawn.

It wouldn't be an escape to the Lakes without a spot of messing about on the water. Knotts End has its own jetty if you want to bring your own kayak or stand-up paddleboard, and a rowing boat is tied up ready for guests to take on a jaunt on the lake. Swimmers can hop in straight from the jetty to explore the shoreline, or sign up with a local company called Swim the Lakes for a guided swim to one of Ullswater's further-flung islands.

The Boathouse's little corner of the lake is a feast for the senses in all seasons. In autumn, the water is at its warmest to tempt wild swimmers, and the hills across the shore are a blaze of russet-hued heather. In winter, when snow caps the peaks (and may even fall on the shoreline and jetty), The Boathouse is a toasty place in which to hole up, feed the fire and watch the stars come out. The arrival of spring sees the swans that bob around the lake with their cygnets, and the surrounding woodland carpeted with bluebells. Whichever season you choose for a journey to Ullswater, you won't need much convincing that you've arrived at one of the wonders of the world.

On the doorstep

Admire Aira Force: Do go chasing waterfalls – Aira is a force of nature, a dramatic rushing waterfall that cascades for 20m (65ft) into a wooded glen cared for by the National Trust and reachable by foot from Ullswater. Admire its power from the higgledy-piggledy staircases that follow it down.

Hike Helvellyn: Experienced hikers shouldn't miss one of the most wildly beautiful hikes in Britain – Helvellyn mountain via Striding Edge. This 8-mile/5–7-hour trek is a scrambly challenge, winding up the sharp and vertiginous spine of Striding Edge to the summit (at 950m/3,116ft, Helvellyn is England's third highest peak) and down again via Swirral Edge to Glenridding, on the banks of Ullswater.

Wild *Escapes*

Opposite: The Boathouse on the shore of Ullswater.

Bottom left: Inside the boathouse.

Bottom right: The boathouse comes with its own jetty, perfect for enjoying the views with a morning cup of coffee.

Wild *Escapes*

Woodlands

Into the woods

'Between every two pines is a doorway to a new world', wrote naturalist John Muir; words to ponder next time you wander under the cool canopy of a tall tree. Forests cover 30 per cent of our planet's surface, acting as the Earth's lungs, as homes to millions of living things and as barriers to climate change. We depend on them for our very survival. They are ancient and long-standing, yet intricately alive in ways we're only just learning about. *The Hidden Life of Trees* by Peter Wohlleben beautifully explores how trees are living, connected beings, sharing nutrients, passing messages and creating their own intricate ecosystems. So perhaps it's no surprise that these bosky landscapes make wonderful places to explore.

In our busy, built-up world, peaceful woodlands are the perfect places to slow down and practise mindfulness. Next time you stand 'between two pines', John Muir style, try the Japanese art of shinrin-yoku. Also known as forest bathing, shinrin-yoku involves standing among trees, calming your mind and connecting your senses to the forest around you. The Japanese have been practising forest bathing since the 1980s, believing it combats stress and anxiety. It's definitely an easy way to slow a busy brain and reconnect with the natural world – and it's completely free. Walk into the woods in Llanerchaeron in Ceredigion, Wales (see page 143), slow your breathing and your senses will start to pick up the wonders of different seasons – bright flashes of wood anemones and bluebells on the forest floor below, chirruping redstarts, goldcrests and nuthatches in the branches above. Can you hear birdsong, the sound of the wind in branches, the scurrying of a squirrel? Can you smell fresh green things growing and the richness of the loam under your feet? Can you feel the rough bark under your fingers?

British forests feel like timeless places – but only 2.5 per cent of our forests are classed as 'ancient', dating from 1600 or before. To ramble among trees that have seen endless kings and queens, times of war and peace, come and go, there's nowhere quite like the New Forest in Hampshire. This national park has an ironic name, given that it began life as a royal hunting ground back in 1079. Almost a thousand years later, it's home to thickets of ancient oak and yews, interspersed with open moorland. Wild ponies and donkeys roam free here, and may even come to say hello (and to investigate your picnic) if you stop for a while on a walk.

Each and every forest tells a story, but some also inspire literary favourites. Angling Spring Wood, near Great Missenden in the Chilterns, is a small but beautiful bluebell-carpeted place where author Roald Dahl used to ramble – and where he came up with the idea for his much-loved story, *Fantastic Mr Fox*. In autumn, this ancient cluster of beech and hornbeam is a blaze of russets and golds,

> **Slow your breathing and your senses will start to pick up the wonders of different seasons – bright flashes of wood anemones and bluebells on the forest floor below, chirruping redstarts, goldcrests and nuthatches in the branches above.**

*Below: Woodland path next
to the Roundhouse at Blickling.*

*Right (both): Exploring the woodland
at Warcleave Cottage.*

and best of all, this magical wild spot is only an hour from central London by train, making a woodland escape easy if the only tall things you usually see are skyscrapers.

Some of our trees have also witnessed key moments in history. There's the Martyr's tree in Tolpuddle, Dorset, where the Trade Union movement was born, and Sir Isaac Newton's apple tree at Woolsthorpe Manor, Lincolnshire – possibly the oldest apple tree in the world, and which helpfully demonstrated the force of gravity to its resident.

We have a lot to thank trees for. They aren't just a shady haven – trees are the ultimate carbon capture

and storage machines. Like huge sinks, woods and forests absorb atmospheric carbon and lock it up for centuries. They have the potential to tackle the climate change crisis – and the National Trust aims to help by planting 20 million trees across the UK, as part of its ambitions to create new homes for wildlife, protect landscapes prone to flooding and to aid in the fight against climate change. You can even plant your own tree, to add to the numbers of saplings springing up at Trust sites across Britain.

The next time you feel like you need grounding, connect with your inner forest dweller and seek out a friendly tree. After all, most of them have weathered far more storms than we have.

Warcleave Cottage, Devon

'Come to the woods, for here is rest. There is no repose like that of the green, deep woods,' wrote naturalist John Muir, and it makes a fitting invitation to the calming presence of Warcleave Cottage. If you ever made a den among the trees as a child, you'll feel right at home at this woodsy house, where a tall, tree-top balcony gives glimpses towards Dartmoor's rolling open heathland.

The living is easy at Warcleave Cottage. The kitchen, bathroom and two bedrooms are all located on the same floor, along with a bright and airy open-plan living and dining space. Slide open the balcony windows and curl up within the tips of the trees, looking out at the River Teign and the enticingly wild moors beyond. Two pale-hued bedrooms are simply furnished to allow the green leaves that frame their windows to take centre stage. At the bottom of the garden, the river bubbles and burbles its way towards the sea, and its banks are alive with the delicate mauve seep of bluebells each spring. A grassy lawn with a wide picnic table lets you start slowly on sunny mornings, with a cuppa after a forest bathe right in front of the cottage.

If you ever made a den among the trees as a child, you'll feel right at home at this woodsy house, where a tall, tree-top balcony gives glimpses towards Dartmoor's rolling open heathland

You're inside the northern tip of Dartmoor National Park at Warcleave, and surely there's no landscape in Britain that packs so much into such a walkable space. Dartmoor, at only 20 miles in length and width, is one of the country's smaller national parks, but is home to mile upon mile of open moorland and gnarled ancient oak woodland that feel truly wild. There are 160 stone tors to clamber over, 1,500 boisterous native ponies nosing about and, astonishingly, the remains of no less than 5,000 Bronze Age settlements. A network of 450 miles of public trails to hike, bike or horse ride along will keep all kinds of explorer happy.

Back at the cottage, a gaggle of ghosts and ghoulies (as well as fairies and piskies) may inspire spine-prickling stories told by the fire on chilly winter nights. Have you heard of the Hairy Hands, who haunt the narrow lanes around Postbridge and attempt to pull motorists off the road? And only the bravest of hikers should climb Hound Tor – they say this rocky outcrop was once a pack of hunting hounds, turned to stone forever because they knocked over a witches' cauldron on a hunt. If all that sounds too spooky, Devon's gentler side is less than an hour away by car. On a summer's day, you'd be forgiven for thinking you were by the Mediterranean on Britain's answer to the French Riviera – the South Devon coast, where swimmers can dip in calm turquoise waters at Ansteys Cove and Maidencombe Beach. Whether you choose rugged moorland or soft sand for a big day out, the woods will beckon you home again come evening, where you can watch the twilight and listen for the hoot of owls from your treetop hideaway.

On the doorstep

Hike to Ponsworthy: Dip into Dartmoor on this rewarding day hike from the moorland town of Chagford to the hamlet of Ponsworthy along the Two Moors Way, a long-distance trail linking Exmoor and Dartmoor. Trek a 13-mile/5–6-hour ribbon of open moorland and lesser-visited tors straight from the cottage door.

A swim and a pub stop at Fingle Bridge: Take a cooling dip in the River Teign, when permitted, where it pools into a wide weir at Fingle Bridge in the Teign Gorge below the Castle Drogo estate. It's a 15-minute drive or a 1½-hour walk from Warcleave Cottage , then warm up in the sunshine in the riverside pub garden at the Fingle Bridge Inn.

Below left (top to bottom): Inside the walls are filled with paintings by former owner, E. C. Lysaught. Sit out on the tree-top balcony, surrounded by woodland.

Below Right: Fingle Bridge, with walking trails along the riverside and an idyllic pub.

Above: Late-summer views over Dartmoor.

Exploring further afield near Haytor.

Wild *Escapes*

The Round House, Suffolk

If you go down to the woods today ... you may stumble upon a fairytale cottage, hidden away in the forests of Suffolk.

The Round House will delight lovers of miniature things – this charmingly spherical cottage is a pocket-sized version of the Rotunda, the grand Italianate manor house on the Ickworth estate, in which the cottage resides. Built in the mid-19th century as a shooting lodge, and later used as a gamekeeper's cottage, the Round House is now a rather elegant and surprisingly spacious holiday home. Three bedrooms – two doubles and a twin – sleep six on the upper floor. Downstairs, you'll find a half-moon sitting room with velvet sofas facing a roaring fire and an airy kitchen complete with an oval wooden table for King Arthur-style feasts (apparently, it was a challenge for National Trust staff to find furniture to fit the house's unique proportions).

It's all rather magical in this little woodland house, reached by its own rough track. The surroundings feel like they were designed by the Brothers Grimm. Close to the cottage is Fairy Lake, a still, reed-lined pond designed, like everything at Ickworth, with bucolic beauty in mind. The cottage also has a shaded porch, a dreamy spot for an early morning cuppa, and its own small garden, where you may spot fallow and muntjac deer nosing among the surrounding thickets.

The Round House is on the edge of Ickworth estate – miles of rolling parkland, as well as Ickworth

Close to the cottage is Fairy Lake, a still, reed-lined pond designed, like everything at Ickworth, with bucolic beauty in mind

House and its elegant gardens, are yours to explore. Flamboyant Ickworth has been described as a 'stupendous monument of folly' – but if it was considered outlandish when first constructed in 1795 by the Hervey family, age has only made this Neo-classical house seem more magnificent with each passing year. Ickworth was finally opened to the public when it was given to the National Trust by the Earl of Bristol in the 1950s, and the Trust has been working to restore the rotunda ever since. The 32-m (105-ft) manor house now plays host to a priceless art collection, with paintings by Velazquez, Titian, Gainsborough and Hogarth lining the walls. Outdoors, the walled garden is a delight – there's even an 'honesty barrow' where you can pick up fresh fruit and vegetables in exchange for a donation, ready to cook back at the Round House.

There are hundreds of acres at Ickworth, criss-crossed with hiking and cycling paths, so there's no need to go far to explore the landscape where 'the ground nobly broke into hill and dale [with] fine hanging woods and lawn', as the Duchess of Northumberland observed in her diary in 1770. There's also the Porter's Lodge café on site, in case you fancy a slap-up cream tea without having to stray far from the cottage's extended back garden.

Ickworth and the Round House, may have been the follies of their day, but today they're here to be admired, explored, stayed in – and taken as reminders that things of beauty are a joy forever.

Wild *Escapes*

On the doorstep

Bike about: Ickworth has its own cycle hire hub, so you can easily grab a set of wheels to explore the estate's miles of parkland trails. Or head out onto Sustrans' route 51 to reach Bury St Edmunds in three miles or even carry on to reach the coast at Felixstowe, 42 miles away.

Ickworth's Off the Beaten Track Trail: This 6½-mile/2-hour walk around the further-flung corners of the estate meanders through ancient woodland of oak and ash where you're likely to stumble across grazing deer. The trail also passes the estate's peaceful church, the walls decorated with 14th-century frescos.

Opposite: The dining area, with the woodland garden beyond.

Above: A redwood tree dappled in light.

Below (left to right): Gateway to the gardens on the Ickworth estate. Morning coffee on the terrace at the Roundhouse. The Rotunda, the main house on the Ickworth estate. The Roundhouse was built as a miniature version of this grand building.

Abermydyr Cottage, Ceredigion

What do Little Red Riding Hood, the Three Little Pigs and Snow White all have in common? These storybook favourites all lived, squirreled away, in that classic trope of children's fairy stories – a perfect Lilliputian cottage, hidden in the woods. And there's a corner of west Wales where a real-life version (minus predatory wolves and the seven dwarves, of course) makes for a folksy escape among the trees.

Peachy-yellow Abermydyr cottage is part of the Llanerchaeron Estate, and was originally home to the coachman of the Lewis family who would tend to their horses. The cottage is pleasingly homely but has surprisingly grand origins – Abermydyr was designed in the early 19th century by John Nash, who went on to establish himself as a great Regency architect, building Buckingham Palace for a rather more illustrious client.

Inside is as cosy as it gets, with wooden floors below, exposed beams above and a wood burner you'll want to keep well-stocked to stay snug on frosty winter days. The sitting room's armchairs centre around the fire, and arched gothic-style windows look out on the surrounding woods. This is a cottage where everyone can relax, too – the downstairs floor at Abermydyr is wheelchair-friendly and includes a twin bedroom with an accessible en-suite shower room. The tallest visitors should take care, though – there are low beams dotted around the house. The kitchen has a double-height ceiling and lots of room for foodies to cook in, and from here wooden steps wind upwards to simple, spic-and-span bedrooms, including one right under the eaves with a decorative iron bedstead that

> **Spend a whole day wandering around the working farm's stockyard, home to Welsh Black cattle and rare-breed Welsh pigs, stroll among 200-year-old fruit trees in the walled gardens or get lost in the woods**

Sleeping Beauty would have been proud to call her own.

Wrap up warm – there are wonders on the doorstep. You are on the banks of the River Aeron and surrounded by the sprawling Llanerchaeron Estate, free to wander in the acres of walled gardens, parklands and farmland that surround the main house, an elegant Georgian villa in John Nash's signature stately style that has stood remarkably unaltered for over 200 years. You could easily spend a whole day wandering around the working farm's stockyard, home to Welsh Black cattle and rare-breed Welsh pigs, stroll among 200-year-old fruit trees in the walled gardens or get lost in the woods, where different seasons bring fleeting wonders – wild daffodils, wood anemones and bluebells on the forest floor, and redstarts, goldcrests and nuthatches in the branches above. Keen joggers should aim to stay here over a weekend – Llanerchaeron hosts its own Parkrun event every Saturday morning at 9am, a lovely way to explore the grounds.

For a big dose of fresh air, blow the cobwebs away by the sea. The Ceredigion coast is less than 10 minutes' drive away, where the colourful coastal town of Aberaeron gives way to a wild coastline of coves, caves and cliff-top walks. Further along the coast, the National Trust's Mwnt beach is an especially wonderful spot, where verdant cliffs stop suddenly high above a sheltered cove of apricot sand. Bottlenose dolphins are often spotted jumping for joy out to sea here, and it's a magical place to spend a sunny day before swapping waves for woodland and meandering back under the trees to your storybook sanctuary.

On the doorstep

Llanerchaeron riverside trail: Ramble along the banks of the Aeron from the cottage all the way to reach the sea. This flat, 3-mile/1-hour woodland stroll ends where the river meets the ocean in Aberaeron in Cardigan Bay.

Penbryn Beach: This sweep of silky sand backed by green cliffs, cared for by the National Trust, is a wonderful place to spot dolphins out at sea or take a salty dip (friendly seals may come and see what you're up to). Penbryn is a 30-minute drive from Abermydyr.

Opposite (top to bottom): Abermydyr Cottage nestled in the trees. The walled garden at Llanerchaeron.

Above: Welsh blankets warm the bedrooms upstairs.

Below: In late summer, the cottage garden is full of blackberries. Buy apples grown on the estate and make a hearty crumble.

Wild Escapes

Cartref, Gwynedd

Yr Wyddfa, or Mount Snowdon, is Wales's loftiest and most famous peak. Its 1,085-m (3,560-ft) summit is visited by more than half a million hikers a year. It's also one of the country's most fabled mountains; this is where King Arthur slayed Rhitta, a terrible giant who created a cape for himself out of the beards of his enemies. Rhitta's corpse was covered in huge stones by Arthur's men and hidden at the summit. Yr Wyddfa means 'the tomb' in English – these days, Rhitta's resting place is topped by a less macabre trig point, offering some of the finest mountain panoramas in Britain.

If you're planning to take on the great mountain – or explore the other peaks in this rugged corner of north Wales – you'll find a wonderful walkers' base waiting in the foothills. At first glance, you'd be forgiven for mistaking wood-clad Cartref for a glorified shed – this simple cabin is just the spot for a back-to-basics stay. What's on an epic scale here is the surrounding landscape. You're among moss-clad trees in a pocket of woodland on Hafod Y Llan, a working farm, with a tinkling brook running right below the cottage. There's no garden to speak of, but outdoor seating outside the cabin offers views of the far-off peaks, guaranteed to tempt you to lace up your boots.

Right on the doorstep of the cabin is the Watkin Path, one of six routes up Yr Wyddfa (the other five are the Llanberis Path, the Pyg Track, the Miners' Track, the Rhyd Ddu Path and the Snowdon Ranger Path), is often considered the most challenging. In four miles and almost 1,000m (3,300ft) of ascent, it'll whisk you up to the summit via the mountain's scree-lined southern slopes. Pick a clear day for the trek if you can – eagle eyes can spot an astonishing 24 counties, 29 lakes and 17 islands from the peak, with views reaching across England, Scotland, Ireland and the Isle of Man, making Britain look like a pocket map spread out all around you.

Once you're back on level ground, Cartref is there waiting, wonderfully warm and inviting. Inside is just as dinky as the outside. There's a dining-cum-sitting room with a tiny table for two, plus a squashy sofa, wooden floor and big window make this space feel surprisingly airy and modern. The galley kitchen looks out at surrounding trees and mossy boulders, and is kitted out with a fridge, a hob and a microwave for simple suppers.

The bedroom fits a double bed and not much else, but this will seem like heaven to sink into after a long day in the blustery hills, and with the window open, the waterfall that rushes over the rocks outside can lull you to sleep. The cabin's size means there's no indoor shower – but step outside and there's a copper bath tub waiting on the decking for an alfresco wash with waterfall views. Yes, Cartref is small – but its doll's-house proportions are charming, and if you're used to roughing it in bothies or shivering in your tent after a hike, this cabin in the woods makes for a seriously cosy haven after a long day on high, searching for Yr Wyddfa's secrets.

> Cartref's doll's-house proportions are charming - if you're used to roughing it in bothies or shivering in your tent after a hike, this cabin makes for a cosy haven

On the doorstep

Carneddau mountain range: Have you stood tall on Yr Wyddfa and want to venture further afield? The Carneddau range is a summit-bagger's dream, with 20 peaks measuring over 600m (2,000ft) in height. Carnedd Llewelyn and Carnedd Dafydd, Wales second- and third-highest peaks respectively, can be tackled together in a challenging 9-mile/6-hour loop that begins a 20-minute drive from Cartref.

Betws y Coed: This pretty stone village, meaning 'prayer house in the woods', is a 15-minute drive from Cartref. It's a great adventure hub – mountain biking trails climb straight from the village into the surrounding forests, and there's a clutch of outdoor shops and inviting pubs.

View of a waterfall and mountains on the Watkin Path up to Yr Wyddfa (Snowdon).

Opposite (left to right): Simple and stylish living room at Cartref. Look out onto the waterfall from the kitchen window. Moss-covered logs in the woodland surrounding the cabin.

Wild *Escapes*

The Lazy T, North Yorkshire

Wondering where the wild things are? Set your compass to the North York Moors, stay a while at the Lazy T and you might just find them. At Tylas Farm (that's the 'T' in Lazy T), you can choose whether to stay on or off the grid in a cosy cottage, two safari-style dome tents (Creekside and Beck) or a tempting wooden cabin (Brook). The hideaways, built using timber from the coppices of mountain ash that surround the farm, are tucked among the trees on raised wooden decking, and the newest member of the gang, Creekside, is also wheelchair accessible.

Each cabin or tent sleeps two or three explorers (or you could take over the whole site with a gaggle of friends), and all are delightfully cosy in any season – think steaming hot showers, huge wooden beds, outdoor kitchens and fire pits where you can cook up some supper over the flames. Brook, named for the babbling stream at the bottom of the valley, has big windows you can fling open on sunny days, and a wood burner to keep you snug on the frostiest mornings. Have a wild wash – the outdoor shower is so close to the surrounding trees that you can reach out and touch green leaves even as you scrub.

This land has been left to rewild itself over recent years, and as a result is bursting with life – keep an eye out for deer, otters, foxes and the birds that sing and hunt for food among the trees. Singing for your own supper is all part of the experience at the Lazy T – the surrounding woodland is rich in edible wild food. Owner Katy will be your foraging guide during your stay – she grew up on this very site and knows like the back of her hand the fresh wild greens of spring and the mushrooms that emerge from the woodland floor when the leaves start to turn. In early autumn, follow her on a foraging foray to hunt for wild food before rustling up a supper of nettle flatbreads, gooseberry ketchup and greens freshly picked from the kitchen garden, served with gathered mushrooms such as ceps and birch boletes, all washed down with spruce tea and elderberry cordial.

> This land has been left to rewild itself over recent years, and as a result is bursting with life – keep an eye out for deer, otters, foxes and the birds that sing and hunt for food among the trees

Be sure to stay up past bedtime – the Lazy T lies in an International Dark Sky Reserve (the North York Moors, one of just 18 in the world), and low levels of light pollution mean that on clear nights you'll see thousands of stars pricking the velvet-black sky. The decking that surrounds the cabins and tents is the perfect place to light a fire, wrap up in a blanket and have a go at spotting Cassiopeia, Orion, Sirius and their friends as they twinkle above you.

On the doorstep

Foraging and supper clubs: Katy offers guided foraging walks of the forests and fields around the Lazy T – learn about plant identification and how to cook with wild edibles, followed by a foraged feast of a picnic or a wild supper club.

Ramble around Rievaulx: A 4-mile/1¼-hour circular walk from the Lazy T takes you to the ruined walls of Rievaulx Abbey, once one of England's most powerful Cistercian monasteries and now a cluster of soaring arches open to the air. The Lazy T will send you off in the right direction with an illustrated map.

Brook, one of several glamping options at the Lazy T, it features a cosy fireplace and outdoor shower amongst the trees.

Trees, Cumbria

'There is something delicious about writing the first words of a story. You never quite know where they'll take you,' said Beatrix Potter. Perhaps your own story should start here in the Lake District, in a log cabin hidden in leafy woodland above the dramatic landscape that the children's author and conservationist loved best.

The property's name (short for Trees Beyond the Fields) is very apt – a log house perched on the side of a Cumbrian fell with tall trees flanking every side. It's the closest you'll get to feeling like you're tucked up in a treehouse without having to leave the ground; although 'Lakes' would have been another say-what-you-see moniker for this hideaway – the cottage has sweeping views of Lake Windermere, sparkling blue and dotted with sailing boats in fine weather, and iron grey with waves lapping the shore when a storm sets in.

High up above the water and not far from Ambleside, Trees is a 1930s log cabin that looks more Canadian than Cumbrian. Inside this eyrie, the sitting room's low-beamed ceiling makes things feel extra cosy, and the small wood burner warms the cockles in the winter. The 1950s-style kitchen is charming too – vintage green window frames look out at leaf-laden branches, making you feel like you are inside the forest, even when you're just making a cup of tea. The two bedrooms are simple but comfortable (one double and one twin make the cabin ideal for a family escape), and the bathroom's walls are lined with exposed wooden beams.

> The closest you'll get to feeling like you're tucked up in a treehouse without having to leave the ground

In the event of rain, Trees' dining room has big French windows that provide expansive views of the Cumbrian landscape and create a sense of space without having to leave the cabin. If the sun shines, the windows fold back completely, creating an indoor-outdoor space perfect for a lazy supper on the balcony with a view of the water. If you're sitting outside of an evening, keep your eyes peeled – wild deer occasionally wander past, and at dawn or dusk you may glimpse the russet flash of a fox.

There's no garden at Trees, so make the lake below you your aquatic back garden for adventures. Windermere, the largest natural lake in England at 10 miles long, has plenty of room for playing Swallows and Amazons. Watersports lovers can store boats and kayaks in the cabin's garage, or you can hire canoes and stand-up paddleboards from nearby Low Wray or at Fell Foot park on the southern tip of the lake. This western side of the lake is ideal if you fancy a swim, too, as the water here is shallower and less busy with boats – Waterhead End is a good jumping-off point for a dip.

This is Beatrix Potter country – her former farmhouse, Hill Top, now cared for by the National Trust, is close by, and two of her favourite lakes, Esthwaite Water, which inspired her froggy character of Jeremy Fisher, and Moss Eccles Tarn, where Potter kept her rowing boat, are also a stroll away. Wherever you explore, the feeling of peace, the local wild things, and the sweeping views from the windows of the cabin are guaranteed to inspire you.

On the doorstep

Beatrix Potter's farmhouse: Hill Top is just over 10 minutes' drive or a 1½-hour walk away, and tells the story of the author, her love for the Lakes and the magical worlds she created. Stroll around the famous vegetable patch where Peter Rabbit had his infamous adventures.

Hike: From Trees, it's a 2-mile/¾-hour walk to reach Latterbarrow Hill's far-reaching views of the fells, and under four miles/1–2 hours to the shores of Esthwaite Water and onwards to Hill Top. From here you can wander back to the cabin through the woodlands of Claife Heights, stopping at Claife Viewing Station, a delightful 18th-century folly with stained glass windows and panoramic vistas.

Opposite: Cosy cabin interiors, with views out to the surrounding woodland.

Left: Windows in the conservatory-style dining space, which leads onto the tree-top balcony.

Right: Dappled light shines on the cabin, surrounded by woodland.

Faraway Treehouse, Cumbria

'I don't believe in things like that – fairies or brownies or magic or anything. It's old-fashioned.'

'Well, we must be jolly old-fashioned then,' said Bessie. 'Because we not only believe in the Faraway Tree and love our funny friends there, but we go to see them too.'

So begins Enid Blyton's *The Folk of the Faraway Tree*, the story of three children who meet mythical creatures in among the branches of an enchanted tree that stretches high into the sky. It may be a fantasy story for little ones, but there's a corner of north Cumbria where you can recapture the magic of Blyton's books – by holing up in a real-life tree-top hideaway.

Follow a woodland path to a clearing in the trees and you'll stumble upon the Faraway Treehouse. Up a staircase and through a wooden door, branches curl around the ceiling and ivy trails along the beams of this wood-clad cabin on stilts. You'd be forgiven for thinking you were sleeping outdoors in the Treehouse – well, if it wasn't so warm and cosy, thanks to the squat wood burner and blanket-piled double bed. The treehouse is the perfect snug for two grown-ups to share, but there's also room for two children, who will love sleeping in the raised platform above the living area.

You're off-grid at the treehouse, but this definitely doesn't feel like camping – there's a solar-powered fridge and gas hob rings in the neat kitchen, while LED fairy lights illuminate a snug sitting room with views of the trees and beyond. Best of all, a roll-top bath steams in the bathroom by a wide window, so you can watch the birds flit about as you soak. Even magical beings have to eat – in the mornings, pull open the velvet curtains for tea and toast with a view, and come evening, light the grill in the outdoor chimenea to cook up a feast.

Faraway is on a working farm not far from the Scottish Borders, and while you can go and say hello to their resident cows, life back at the treehouse feels totally private and tucked away. Walk in the woods, stroll around the edges of nearby Talkin Tarn or swim in the stream and keep an eye out for 'funny friends' – the foxes and deer who also call this corner of the woods home, and the dragonflies and damselflies who visit the nearby pond.

There are other wonders to discover nearby – the nearest stretch of Hadrian's Wall is 10 minutes' drive away. Running 73 miles from coast to coast near the border of England and Scotland, the wall was built to guard the wild north-west frontier of the Roman Empire in AD 122. Walking this crumbling reminder of Britain's past is a spine-tingling brush with history, allowing you to tread literally in the footsteps of the Romans who guarded it. The National Trust looks after six of the most special miles of the wall – from Sewingshields in the east to Cawfields in the west, including the iconic Sycamore Gap, where the 'Robin Hood tree' from the 1991 film *Robin Hood: Prince of Thieves* stands lonely on guard. Another tree that feels bathed in magic.

> In the mornings, pull open the velvet curtains for tea and toast with a view, and come evening, light the grill in the outdoor chimenea to cook up a feast

Inside the treehouse, built mostly from wood, gives a sense of being part of the woodland around you. The bath, which has eye-line views out to the forest, is a highlight.

Opposite: The kitchen and dining space, which continues the fairy-tale theme.

On the doorstep

Birdoswald Roman Fort: A fort, a turret and a milecastle still stand at Birdoswald, built astride Hadrian's Wall in around the year 130. Once a garrison for 800 men, these atmospheric ruins (plus modern visitor centre), a 25-minute drive from Faraway, are a great place to start if you're planning on hiking in Hadrian's footsteps.

Scale Skiddaw: The northern tips of both the Lake District and the Pennines aren't far from Faraway. For a big day in the hills, climb Skiddaw in the Lakes, just over an hour's drive away. Wainwright called this mountain a 'friendly giant', and the views from its 931-m (3,054-ft) peak, far above Keswick, are pretty gigantic, too.

North Lodge and River Cabin, Aberdeenshire

Is it a tin can, or is it a tiny house? The River Cabin is so compact that it could be considered a hybrid of both. This metal-clad gem watches the river go by from along the tall, susurrating pines, just waiting to be your own little escape into the Scottish wilderness.

The main house here is a short walk away from River Cabin – North Lodge is a roomy, elegant stone cottage in the heart of the Glen Dye Estate that sleeps six. Built in the late 1890s as a home for forest workers, the outside of this Georgian house is fairly traditional, but inside is stuffed with modern art and fascinating objects. There's also a gramophone, for a little boogie in the evening, and a big open fire with a peacock-blue chair facing it, all ready for a nightcap whisky before bed. Up the wooden stairs are three airy bedrooms and two bathrooms, all emblazoned with artworks in bold colours.

Outside and along a little path to the brook is the River Cabin, your own mini hideaway in the woods. Perched on the bank of the River Dye and surrounded by trees, this simple dwelling the shape of a Monopoly house is clad in corrugated sheet metal and is full of books, games and other old-fashioned delights. The outside is the best bit, though – a large green barbeque is there for you to sizzle up a feast and there's a dining table for a lunch with a soundtrack of the burbling

> **When the tub is bubbling away, it's a dreamy place to watch night fall and the stars come out between the tallest tips of the trees**

water. Next to the cabin is the *pièce de résistance*, a Scandi-style hot tub and a big stack of wood ready to fire it up with. When the tub is bubbling away, it's a dreamy place to watch night fall and the stars come out between the tallest tips of the trees – before you wind your way home to bed in North Lodge.

Love to eat local? You'd be hard-pressed to find food with fewer air miles than at Glen Dye, where you can pick your own ingredients in the vegetable garden or stock up on fresh eggs from the estate's chickens. There's even a BYOB 'pub' to hob-nob with other guests, kitted out with a log fire and a record player.

While there's other accommodation dotted among the trees at Glen Dye, you've all got enough elbow room – the house and cabin are surrounded by no less than 6,000ha (15,000 acres) of forest and moorland that feel wild in the truest, Scottish sense. At the Lodge, you're right in the centre of the estate, which is laced with hiking and biking routes that are yours to explore. Here be mountains, too – the towering tor of Clachnaben is calling to be climbed, and the remote Cairn o' Mount mountain pass leads twistingly onwards towards the Highlands. Wild things will feel right at home.

On the doorstep

Climb Clachnaben mountain: Stand tall on this massive granite tor overlooking Glen Dye – it's a 5½-mile/2–3-hour out-and-back hike through woodland and wide valleys before a scramble to the 589m (1,931ft) summit.

Learn a wilderness skill: Glen Dye's outdoor instructors offer all sorts of workshops based on the estate, designed to bring out your inner woodland spirit. Try river swimming, bushcraft, survival skills, foraging and axe throwing.

Opposite (top to bottom): Roam the many walking trails on the Glen Dye estate. Woodland views towards Clachnaben mountain.

Right: The summer cottage by the riverside at Glen Dye.

Below (left to right): The modern interiors at North Lodge. The rustic Glen Dye Arms, a place for guests to relax and meet. Inside the River Cabin.

Moors, Hills & Fells

Hiking the hills

Roaming with a knapsack on your back is one of the simplest and cheapest ways you can enjoy the outdoors on a human-powered adventure. Plus, walking is often the only form of transport that'll allow you to venture into some of the most remote and beautiful pockets of Britain – perhaps that's why there are quite so many poems and songs about the glories of the rambling life.

Walking, hiking, hillwalking – it's hard to define clearcut edges between different kinds of perambulation, except that the walker and the rambler tend to take gentler strolls over rolling countryside with plenty of tea breaks, while the hiker and the hillwalker stride determinedly off into the higher peaks. Walking in mountainous areas in the UK is called hillwalking, or in northern England, including the Lake District and Yorkshire Dales, fellwalking, from the dialect word 'fell' meaning high, uncultivated land. But however challenging you want to make it, a walk is guaranteed to clear your mind, fill your lungs with fresh air and leave you feeling calmer. It'll be worth the blisters.

'Walk through life as though you have something new to learn, and you will,' wrote American philosopher Vernon Howard. There's a simple happiness in the act of placing one foot in front of the other, and walking is as good for you physically as it is mentally. Hiking reduces the risk of disease, strengthens your heart and gives your body a big endorphin boost. It improves memory and attention, and is proven to promote calm thoughts. It's also free (once you own a pair of hiking boots), easy to plan and easy to adapt to levels of fitness and ability – so it's unsurprising that it's one of the most popular ways

> **There's a simple happiness in the act of placing one foot in front of the other, and walking is as good for you physically as it is mentally**

to get outdoors in the UK, with almost three million of us regularly heading out on hiking and hillwalking adventures.

In the late 1700s, the idea of walking for pleasure was popularised by intrepid writers such as Thomas West, who published a guide to England's Lake District in 1778 that piqued the public's interest. Poet William Wordsworth also enjoyed a good stroll and embarked on several walking tours in the UK, immortalised in his poems. The most famous mountain man is, of course, Alfred Wainwright, the father of fellwalking, whose pictorial guides to the Lakeland Fells, compiled in the 1950s and 1960s, are a modern bible for lovers of outdoors.

Women have also paved the way to modern hillwalking – they've just been less well-known. A pioneer of mountaineering was Dorothy Wordsworth, who in 1818, became one of the first people to climb Scafell Pike. She never published her account, though her brother William would later 'borrow' her words for inclusion in his best-selling guide to the Lake District. Around the same time, Ellen Weeton, a governess from Lancashire, was regularly clocking up 35 miles a day on her epic hikes across England and undertook a solo climb of Snowdon in Wales at the age of 48, using her bonnet to protect her from the sight of steep drops down the mountainside.

Even as interest in the magic of the mountains increased, much of the land around industrial cities such as Sheffield and Manchester was still privately owned, and walking on these lands was illegal.

Rambling clubs started popping up in northern England, and early hiking enthusiasts began advocating for the 'right to roam' freely. The country's first rambling club, the Sunday Tramps, was started in 1879. By the 20th century, activists were pushing for legislation to enshrine open access in law. It culminated in the mass trespass of Kinder Scout in 1932, when hundreds of men and women defied the law to walk over hills and moorland to the plateau of Kinder Scout, Derbyshire, in what would go on to become the Peak District National Park. Parliament finally passed the National Parks and Access to the Countryside Act in 1949 and created the Peak District National Park in 1951. We've been a hillwalking nation ever since.

While (legal) hiking and hillwalking are relatively modern pursuits, they're also a wonderful way to connect with our ancient landscapes. To walk in the footsteps of the Romans, just follow the 84 undulating miles of Hadrian's Wall, a fortification that once marked the northernmost extent of the Roman Empire, or go searching for the remains of Sarn Helen, a cobbled Roman route that once crossed Wales from north to south. On the summit of Scafell Pike, you'll find Britain's highest Great War memorial, restored each year by volunteers who camp out on the top of the mountain. Afterwards, head down for a well-earned pint at the welcoming Wasdale Head pub, the birthplace of British rock climbing, at the bottom of the valley. Lovers of legends may want to seek out the spirit of King Arthur on Mount Snowdon – it's said that he once killed a fierce giant, Rhitta Gawr, and buried his remains in the foot of the grandest mountain of Wales.

Even without encounters with giants, mountains and moorlands can be treacherous places if you don't take proper care. Wear suitable clothing and footwear with a treaded sole, and choose warm, windproof and waterproof layers. Carry food, such as high energy snacks, and plenty of water – it's easy to become dehydrated even in cooler weather. A map and compass are essential, and while a fully charged mobile phone should be carried, you may not be able to rely on getting any signal on a mountainside. Check the weather forecast before you go and be prepared to turn back if conditions turn against you.

If you do feel your spirits dampen at the sight of storm clouds, think of words written by Alfred Wainwright: 'The fleeting hour of life of those who love the hills is quickly spent, but the hills are eternal. Always there will be the lonely ridge, the dancing beck, the silent forest; always there will be the exhilaration of the summits. These are for the seeking, and those who seek and find while there is still time will be blessed both in mind and body.'

Hikers walk up Mam Tor in the Peak District.

Bwthyn Mai, Gwynedd

Here be dragons. At Bwthyn Mai, you'll stay right in the heart of a storied landscape, home to some of the myths and legends that have shaped Wales – including the scaly, fire-breathing kind.

A grassy track leads you through the Craflwyn Estate in Eryri to reach this characterful little stone cottage, then winds on, tempting walkers with views of far-off hills. Craflwyn was once a monastery, dating back to AD 1200, and this cottage in the grounds still feels pleasingly cloistered and tucked away in the landscape.

Inside Bwthyn Mai, the star of the snug sitting room is the big wood burner where you can get a crackling fire going on a chilly night that will warm the whole cottage in a jiffy. You'll also find a squashy sofa and fully equipped kitchen. The landing holds a surprise for bookworms – a deep window seat with woodland creatures that makes the perfect bolthole to escape to with a good tale. Outside, a wooden picnic table with far-reaching views across the valley is perfect for lazy suppers on long summer evenings.

Upstairs, the main double bedroom sits tucked up in the eaves, with a skylight above the bed for a spot of stargazing on clear nights. There's a tiny second bedroom that's perfect for a child, and that also boasts lofty views of the light-pollution-free dark skies you'll find in this wild corner of the country.

> This spot is so untouched by modern life that you almost expect to see Merlin emerge to watch the dragons battle once again

Wales is a land rich in mythology – and if you want to get right to its heart, this cottage is the perfect jumping-off point. Dinas Emrys is a short walk away and is where it all began – the story goes that this ancient hill fort is the spot where Merlin the wizard came across the red dragon and watched him defeat the white dragon of the Saxons, thus foretelling the coming of King Arthur. The triumphant red dragon now proudly adorns the Welsh flag – and legend has it he still snoozes in the depths of the hillside today; a warning for those to watch their step when exploring up here.

Far below the ruins of the fort are the glassy dark waters of Llyn Dinas lake. If you're hardy enough to brave the icy depths (this lake is fed by Llyn Glaslyn, said to be the coldest lake in Britain), this is a wonderful place for a wild swim with a panoramic view of Dinas Emrys. This spot is so untouched by modern life that you almost expect to see Merlin emerge to watch the dragons battle once again. It's a magical place, but even the hardiest swimmer will eventually want to head back up the valley to the cosy welcome of Bwthyn Mai, to dry their bathers in front of the fire and warm up with a blanket and a coffee – or a dram of local Welsh spirit in that tempting window nook.

On the doorstep

Dinas Emrys: Conquer the summit of the wooded hill, crowned with an ancient fort, the site of Merlin's legendary encounter with the red dragon. You'll reach the fort after about a 1-mile/30-minute stroll along a trail straight from the cottage door – keep your eyes peeled for the waterfall that feeds Merlin's Pool along the way.

Yr Wyddfa: Up for a challenge? Lofty Yr Wyddfa, the highest peak in England and Wales at 1,085m (3,560ft), is practically outside your door at Bwthyn Mai. The strenuous Watkin Path zips you up to the summit from the nearby village of Nant Gwynant and back over eight miles, or the less steep, nine-mile Llanberis Path is a 30-minute drive away.

Porthmadog: The sea is just 10 miles from Bwthyn Mai. Watch brightly painted fishing boats bob at the harbour town of Porthmadog, then follow the coast path for a mile/30 minutes to the right to reach the sandy sweep of Borth Y Gest beach, or under 2 miles/1 hour to the left to explore the Italianate village of Portmeirion.

Wild Escapes

Above: Shafts of early morning light in the garden, with mountain views.
Opposite (top to bottom): Llyn Dinas lake nearby. The fairy-tale Bwthyn Mai, with a cosy reading nook inside.

Hafod Y Llan Campsite, Gwynedd

Here's how one happy camper described Hafod Y Llan, a simple campsite spread out in Wales's Nant Gwynant valley in the shadow of Yr Wyddfa: 'Babbling stream, large shady oaks, sheep in an adjacent fold and, of course, mountains and lakes. Want starry skies? This is a superb place to bring your binoculars.' It's hard to think of a more appealing place to pitch your tent.

Hafod Y Llan is big on landscapes – this cluster of fields sits right next to the rushing waters of the Cwm Llan river, which runs up to the base of mighty Yr Wyddfa. Elsewhere, though, simple is the buzzword at this no-frills campsite – you won't find electricity, hot water or a phone signal available, but instead there's a wealth of space, mountain views and peace to luxuriate in. The whole campsite has a 'nearly wild camping' feel that's brilliant for anyone who wants to introduce kids (or fair-weather campers) to the delights of outdoor escapes with a tent, a stove and not much else.

Down to brass tacks – the campsite has a small block with toilets and hot showers, plus cold running water for washing. You'll need to bring your own drinking water, but the village of Beddgelert is an easy 3-mile walk (1½-hours) away if you need to stock up on bits and bobs, and will seem like a cosmopolitan hotspot after a few nights at the campsite, given that it boasts a shop, post office and pub, the homely Tanronnen Inn.

Stay up late enough on clear nights, and millions of stars will start to sprinkle the unpolluted sky above

Cars are parked well away from pitches, giving a slow-paced feel to the campsite, and fire pits are permitted, so you can sit by the welcome warmth of crackling logs on chilly evenings before bed. When you and your fellow campers have turned in for the night, the only noise will be the soothing, far-off rush of the river. Stay up late enough on clear nights, and millions of stars will start to sprinkle the unpolluted night sky above.

Most hikers camp here to test themselves on the biggie – Yr Wyddfa. The steeply ascending Watkin Path leads right from the campsite to the summit over three hefty miles, and if you want to escape the crowds, walking routes also lead to lesser-known Welsh peaks.

For lower-level valley walks, you're right on the National Trust's largest farm – Hafod Y Llan's 1,600ha (4,000 acres) are home to Welsh mountain sheep, Welsh Black cattle and a couple of woolly alpacas. Part of the farm is given over to nature as a Site of Special Scientific Interest, nurturing micro landscapes such as blanket bog, heath and dwarf juniper as well as oak woodlands. You can also ramble along the shores of two tempting lakes – Llyn Dinas, where the foothills of Snowdon are reflected in the glassy water, and Llyn Gwynant, which makes for an invigorating wild swimming spot.

On the doorstep

Climb Crib Goch: Up for a challenge? Experienced scramblers can tackle Crib Goch, a 'knife-edged' arete that soars upwards to Snowdon's summit, right from the campsite. Expect sweeping Snowdonian vistas but a challengingly narrow route on this Grade 1 (scrambles are graded 1-4, and 1 is the easiest) 3½ mile/3-4-hour scramble.

Cwm Idwal walk: This moderate 3-mile/3-hour trek around a glaciated lake is short but it really delivers a treat for the senses – staggering mountains rise on all sides and are reflected in the waters of the oldest National Nature Reserve in Wales, 25 minutes by car from the campsite. Keep an eye out for the Idwal Slabs, climbing routes that have offered a training ground for mountaineers over many decades, including Everest conqueror Sir Edmund Hillary.

Views towards Llyn Gwynant and Eyri mountains from along the Pen Y Pass road.

Above: Pitch your tent next to one of the fire pit areas at Hafod Y Llan, for a cosy evening with fellow campers.

Below (left to right): The nearby village of Beddgellert. Snuggle up in your sleeping bag. The Watkin path leading to the summit of Yr Wyddfa.

Wild Escapes

Dyffryn Mymbyr, Gwynedd

In 1931, a young Thomas Firbank stepped onto Dyffryn Mymbyr, a 970-ha (2,400-acre) sheep farm sprawled across the soaring hills and lush valleys of north Wales. At the age of 21, and with little farming experience, he had just impulsively purchased an area of land as far as the eye could see. What happened next is chronicled in his best-selling novel, *I Bought A Mountain*. In it, Thomas tells of the joys and challenges he and his first wife, Esmé, faced in this corner of the Welsh mountains, as they learned how to run a successful sheep farm with the help of the local community. The story is weaved around the rugged beauty of the surrounding landscape, as well as their love of hillwalking. The pair were keen mountaineers, and the book concludes with the gripping tale of how they and two friends took on the Welsh Three Thousand Challenge – conquering all of Eryri's 15 peaks – in less than nine hours. At the time, breaking the record.

The Firbanks' love for their Eryri home is now a lasting legacy. After Thomas moved away to fight in the Second World War, Esmé stayed at Dyffryn and went on to found the Snowdonia National Park Society, a conservation charity that works with volunteers and local organisations to care for Eryri. On her death in 1991, the farm was bequeathed to the National Trust. You can even spend a night or two on this storied upland farm – a pair of Victorian stone cottages on the estate have been 'rustically restored' and sleep 12 in total, making a roomy base for hiking-mad groups, right in the midst of the Welsh mountains.

The main farmhouse at Dyffryn Mymbyr sleeps eight.

Follow in the Firbanks' footsteps and hike the surrounding peaks straight from your front door

Inside, the sitting room's large picture window overlooks Moel Siabod's green flanks and 872-m (2,860-ft) summit. If the view of the mountain (the name means 'the shapely hill' in Welsh) makes you yearn to get out and stand upon its peak, it's a 6½-mile (2–3-hour) circular hike that starts just down the road in Pont Cyfyng. The dining room is clad in warm oak panelling, and there's a big family kitchen with a farmhouse table ready to crowd around for a hearty feast. The utility room is a brilliant place to stash muddy hiking boots and wet waterproofs. Upstairs, make sure you nab the master bedroom – it has sweeping mountain views. There's another double and two twins, all of which also look out at the peaks, as well as two modern bathrooms.

The smaller cottage is still surprisingly spacious and feels as homely as it must have done in the Firbanks' time. The large sitting room has a traditional inglenook fireplace in pride of place, where now a cheerful wood burner crackles away. Two bedrooms, one twin and one double, are upstairs under thick wooden beams and are irresistibly cosy to tuck up in after a long day out in the elements.

You're more likely to be found outdoors if you're staying at these cottages – you're in the heart of Eryri here, with Yr Wyddfa's ice-tipped Horseshoe beckoning walkers from every window. Follow in the Firbanks' footsteps and hike the surrounding peaks straight from your front door, or walk to the nearby National Mountain Centre to book guided rock climbing, mountain biking and winter mountaineering courses. Don't forget to pack your copy of *I Bought a Mountain*, so you can get lost in Thomas's lyrical descriptions as you explore.

On the doorstep

Tryfan: To experience Eryri grandeur without the crowds that gather on its namesake mountain, tackle Tryfan's 917-m (3,008-ft) peak instead. The scrambly summit is a 6-mile/3–4-hour hike from Dyffryn Mymbyr, where you'll be rewarded with views that Everest climber George Mallory called 'magnificent'.

Explore Llyn Padarn: The lively town of Llanberis, 20 minutes away by car, is home to Snowdonia Watersports, who hire out paddleboards and kayaks and offer guided wild swimming in the deep, calm glacial waters of Llyn Padarn. Paddle with a backdrop of the distant Glyderau and Eryri mountain ranges that the Firbanks loved so much.

Left: Hiking shoes on the slate doorstep of the cottage.

Above: Two cottages sit next to each other, alone on the mountainside, perfect for big groups.

Right: Dffryn Mymber offers views of Yr Wyddfa in the distance.

The Lodges at Longshaw Estate, Derbyshire

This is a tale of two cottages – Yarncliff Lodge and White Edge Lodge, in the heart of the Dark Peak. And you can thank the good folk of Sheffield for the chance to visit them and their surrounding glorious swathe of Peak District moorland and hillside. Longshaw Estate, the former shooting estate of the Duke of Rutland, and where both cottages are nestled, was purchased by the people of Sheffield and donated to the National Trust in 1931, to be enjoyed by all.

You'll find the larger cottage, Yarncliff Lodge, half-hidden among the trees at the western edge of Longshaw. A former estate worker's lodge, this solid stone cottage sleeps six, with plenty of room to spread out across a cosy sitting room, a flagstone-floored kitchen, a handy boot room and three bedrooms looking over Yarncliff Wood and Padley Gorge's gnarled oak trees. Yarncliff is a smart choice for those using public transport to travel around Britain's beauty spots – there's a bus stop right at the end of the driveway and Grindleford train station is a mile down the road in the nearby village of Nether Padley, making this an easy pick if you want country vibes without bringing the car along.

In the east of the estate, White Edge Lodge is immersed in the surrounding moorland, and looks like a tiny castle from afar. Once a gamekeeper's cottage, this stone tower has kept its charm, with exposed brick walls, wooden beams and an arch-ceilinged kitchen cleverly built into what was once a game cellar. The best view of all is upstairs, where a massive roll-top bath looks out over 20 miles of hills and dales, so you can toast the landscape you've explored on foot with a glass of wine after a day out and about.

In autumn, when the heather turns purple, mists hang low around the lodges and red deer can be spotted on the moor, this landscape feels truly wild

The surrounding Hope Valley is a walker's paradise, with trails leading to the Dark Peak, through ancient woodlands and onto open moorland. In autumn, when the heather turns purple, mists hang low around the lodges and red deer can be spotted on the moor, this landscape feels truly wild. Hike Big Moor for big views, walk Mam Tor's undulating edge, search for tumbling waterfalls in Padley Gorge and test your climbing mettle at Froggatt Edge. The pretty village of Grindleford is a short distance away, with two country pubs to choose from mid-adventure, or delve into the tragic history of nearby Eyam, the 'plague village' that provides a fascinating insight into how the Black Death ravaged Britain in the 17th century. Then make the pilgrimage up to Millstone Edge in time for sunset, to watch the evening sky illuminate this dramatic piece of the Peaks in all its golden glory.

Wild *Escapes*

On the doorstep

Climb Froggatt Edge: A slabby gritstone cliff with jaw-dropping views, Froggatt, a 3-mile/1¼-hour stroll from the Longshaw Estate, is a veritable climber's playground of trad routes, with plenty of bouldering options too. No head for heights? A 6-mile/2½–3-hour circular hike takes it all in without you having to dangle from the end of a rope.

Wild swim at Calver Weir: Don a wetsuit for a fresh dip in the River Derwent where it flows into a wide pool above Calver Weir, a 4-mile/1–2-hour hike from Longshaw. The ever-icy water in this shady spot is perfect for a swim if you need to cool down fast during the dog days of summer.

Opposite: Looking out onto the Dark Peak from inside White Edge Lodge.
Above: Nearby Froggart Edge is a climber's paradise. Longshaw Estate is a great natural playground for families to explore.

Upper Booth Campsite, Derbyshire

On 24 April 1932, hundreds of young hikers trespassed on Kinder Scout. They came from all corners to walk on the highest point in the Peak District, then privately owned and used for grouse shooting, to petition for the right to ramble freely over the open country that they loved. One of the most successful acts of civil disobedience in British history, the Kinder Scout Mass Trespass helped to bring about the National Parks and Access to the Countryside Act of 1949, opening up England's wildest landscapes to the masses, and paving the path for the creation of the Pennine Way, the country's first National Trail. Today, Kinder's 636-m (2,086-ft) plateau is a wild spot, to which all outdoor lovers should make a pilgrimage once in their lives. And it's hard to imagine a more perfect place for hikers to camp after such a trek than Upper Booth Farm, a simple campsite hemmed in on all sides by the green hills of the Peaks.

Wander down a narrow lane at the foot of the hills and the landscape opens up into two grassy fields – welcome to Upper Booth Farm. It should be said straight off the bat that this is a simple and no-frills campsite; glampers eager for wood burners and proper beds should pitch up elsewhere. But if simplicity is your thing and you're here to get some mileage under your belt, Upper Booth will be your tented sanctum. Both sides of the National Park – the dramatic Dark Peak to the north and the softer contours of Light Peak in the south – are within walking distance, and the tantalising Pennine Way runs pretty much past your tent pegs.

The campsite is open from April to November, a generous season that allows for crisp, cool hikes in autumn, when you might wake up to frost glistening on your tent. But first, pick your pitch. The upper field has stunning views and pitches laid out around its edges, with dedicated spots for campervans. The lower field has a wash block with lashings of hot water – a boon when you're bone-tired (or bone-chilled) from the mountains and need to warm up. There's good news for four-legged hikers, too – dogs are welcome here at Upper Booth, and both fields are now car free.

The Pennine Way, the 268-mile trail that ranges over the spine of northern England to the Scottish Borders, runs like a ribbon through the yard of the farm that houses the campsite. Head west for a mile to the steep-stepped path of Jacob's Ladder. An 8-mile (3–4-hour) circular trek follows in the footsteps of the trespassers up to Kinder Scout.

It's hard to imagine a more perfect place for hikers to camp after such a trek than Upper Booth Farm

If you're more of a pub walker than a peak-bagger, it's just over a mile east across the fields to reach The Rambler Inn in Edale, which knows its clientele, and serves up a rib-sticking menu of old-school pub grub. Open fires aren't permitted in the Peak District National Park, but the campsite allows barbeques in the Upper Field to satisfy its hungry hikers. Upper Booth also does a fine line in breakfast sarnies on weekend mornings, as well as selling handy BBQ packs, so you don't need to worry too much about what to whip up post-walk. They say food always tastes best eaten outside – after a dazzling day in the hills and with views of the Peaks on all sides, it's bound to be a memorable feast at Upper Booth. Don't forget to raise a glass to the hundreds of men and women who defied the law near this spot, to champion the right for everyone to roam free.

On the doorstep

Castleton Caverns: The pretty village of Castleton is home to a clutch of curious caves – explore the Peak Cavern, the largest natural cave entrance in Britain, which hides under the ruins of Peveril Castle, and Treak Cliff Cavern, with its spindly stalactites (and mites) as well as boundless views of the Hope Valley.

Walk the Pennine Way: To walk England's first National Trail – all 268 miles of it – takes around 18 days, covering swathes of Derbyshire, the Peak District and the Yorkshire Dales on its way to Scotland. It's challenging and remote but endlessly rewarding, and great campsites such as Upper Booth are dotted along the route.

Sunrise views from Mam Tor looking down on Hope Valley, a favourite spot for photographers.

Opposite (left to right): Sheep occasionally wonder into camp at Upper Booth. The Pennine way runs past the campsite. The beautiful vistas of the Edale valley.

Bird How, Cumbria

It takes a lot to leave the beaten track behind you these days. The average UK adult spends half of their waking hours in front of a screen, 83 per cent of us in Britain live cheek by jowl in busy cities and, globally, a staggering 294 billion emails are sent each day. It's enough to give anyone a technology headache. But there's a corner of the Lake District where you can properly leave all that behind and get back to what matters.

Seekers of luxurious stays should read no further and turn to another page. If, however, you love the idea of a truly remote escape and don't mind if it's a little rough around the edges, make a beeline for Bird How.

It's an adventure in itself to reach this romantically remote cottage. Bird How is in the Eskdale valley, a far-off and wild corner of the Lake District with undulating mountain roads that can be cut off completely in winter conditions. Once you've made it this far, you'll rattle down a rough farm track to the cottage – not recommended for low-slung vehicles and is best avoided after dark. When you finally arrive at this former cow barn, you'll be greeted by no phone, no Wi-Fi, no TV signal – no mod cons at all. But what you do get here in spades is a wonderful, wide-open sense of space and of connection to the natural world.

Inside is simple – more bothy than posh cottage – but the sitting room at Bird How has cheery tartan chairs, books and games and an open fire clad in stone. Everything's on one level here, with the shippon (the old cow shed) on the floor below. The kitchen has all the kit you need to cook a proper supper (best to bring everything with you – popping out to the shops for milk is no easy feat) and the bedrooms, one twin and one with bunkbeds, are good for a group of hiking-mad friends to share.

In front of the cottage is a small and rather knobbly grassy garden with a picnic table, and which you're likely to share with a flock of sheep. Noticed something missing from this description? Correct: Bird How doesn't have a bathroom. Wash hands in the kitchen, and brave nipping outdoors to use the Elsan lavatory (a basic chemical toilet found in caravans and boats), tucked underneath the cottage in the old cattle shed.

It's an adventure in itself to reach this romantically remote cottage

It's good fun to disconnect and live a more laid-back life at Bird How, but what's truly dazzling here is the surrounding landscape. Rising right behind the cottage are the foothills of Scafell Pike, which turn a rich russet in autumn and provide hikers with a crowd-free route to the summit of England's highest peak. At the bottom of the field below the cottage runs the River Esk, providing a calming soundtrack of tumbling water. And Hardknott Pass, notorious as the steepest road in England, is a 1½-mile (45-minute) walk or a cycle away if you want to test your mettle on its hairpin bends and 30 per cent gradients. Hike your heart out, then warm the cockles with a hot chocolate by the fire back at Bird How, and feel half a world away.

On the doorstep

Hardknott Roman Fort: There are some places in Britain where you can walk among ruins and feel history rising up all around you – Hardknott Roman Fort, halfway up the pass that shares its name, is one of them. Founded under Hadrian's rule in the 2nd century, the remains of Roman structures at this lonely hillside fort include the commandant's house and the old bath house, now left open to the elements (and to inquisitive hikers).

Scafell Pike: Meet England's highest mountain – at 978m (3,208ft), Scafell is no small feat for hikers to tackle even in the milder weather of summer. Walk its lesser-known Mickledore ascent right from your door at Bird How – it's a 12-mile (7–8-hour) trek up to the summit and back.

Below left: Clean off your hiking boots in the outdoor seating area.

Below right: The roads to the cottage are winding and remote, giving an even greater sense of wildness.

Above left: Views from the cottage onto the mountains of the Eskdale Valley.

Right: From every direction from the cottage, you can see rolling hills, mountains and woodland.

Wild *Escapes*

Eilean Shona, Inner Hebrides

'A wild rocky romantic island it is too', wrote Scottish children's author J. M. Barrie of Neverland, 'it almost taketh the breath away to find so perfectly appointed a retreat on these wild shores.'

Peter Pan's fictional island home, inhabited by mermaids and fairies and threatened by pirates, isn't real of course, but there's somewhere in Britain where you can come pretty close. Eilean Shona, an island on Loch Moidart on the west coast of Scotland, is the real-life place that inspired Barrie's story of the Boy Who Never Grew Up. Barrie spent the summer of 1920 here, exploring in the company of Michael Llewelyn Davies and his brothers, who were immortalised as the original Lost Boys in Barrie's famous story. The island is now privately owned, but nine holiday cottages scattered across its hills, pine groves and rocky coastline are available for week-long escapes – so anyone can journey to Eilean Shona by boat to stay off-grid and reconnect with their own imagination.

There are nine cottages on Eilean Shona, all tucked into their own glades or little valleys, many with windows facing the ocean. The cottages are a blend of comfort and back-to-basics living – with coal fires, big cosy beds, roll-top baths and modern art on the walls, but without electricity or heating, let alone Wi-Fi or Netflix. If you're a fan of the mod cons, this is not the escape for you, but if you like the idea of stepping into the past, where you chop your own wood, cook on a gas stove and go to bed when it's dark (or stay up to read by candlelight), Eilean Shona makes for a return to slow, mindful habits.

> **Peter Pan's island home, inhabited by mermaids and fairies and threatened by pirates, isn't real of course, but there's somewhere in Britain where you can come pretty close**

You're committed to holing up on the island for a week if you stay here. A boat will hop you from the Scottish mainland to Eilean Shona and that's the last you'll see of an engine – there are no vehicles or tarmacked roads; to reach the cottages, you'll follow grassy tracks and coastal paths on foot. The lack of noise and people on Eilean Shona (which means 'sea island' in Scottish Gaelic) makes it a wildlife haven – seals loll on rocks, red deer hide in bracken and eagles circle in the distance.

The cottages are lit by the warm glow of lamps and have wood stoves that will also heat your bath water. Bedrooms are filled with art and colour, and kitchens have everything you need to cook up a hearty supper (or cheat and buy a venison casserole from the island's small but well-stocked shop). It's hard to play favourites, but the Red Cottage, with views of the loch for bird-spotting, and Shepherd's Cottage, hidden down its own remote track, are special picks.

'Of all the delectable islands the Neverland is the snuggest and most compact', wrote Barrie, and it's true that Eilean Shona isn't big – you can walk around it in an hour or so. It's surprisingly varied, though, with thick woodland, craggy coves home to colonies of seals and its own Marilyn (a peak over 150m/500ft) to conquer – Beinn a' Bhaillidh, at 265m (840ft) high. If you feel like making friends, the former village hall is now Eilean Shona's social hub, where there's a weekly 'pub night' as well as a stash of board games, books and table tennis. There's also a little artists' studio on the shore – ideal for spending a day capturing what Barrie called Neverland's 'astonishing splashes of colour'.

On the doorstep

Walk round the island: A varied and rewarding path hugs the coast of Eilean Shona. In some places, it's a wide track through shady woodland, in others you're basically scrambling over the rocky shore, but it's well worth the adventure – especially when you come across secret coves where you can go for a spine-tingling wild swim.

Kayak to a castle: Kayaks are available to rent locally, and you can paddle the short distance across the South Channel to explore Castle Tioram, which sits in splendour on its own tidal island.

Opposite: Interior designs vary between the cottages on Eliean Shona, but are often inspired by bright, warm colours and artwork from around the world.

Above: Views over the loch.

Right: The island has its own boat house, where you can hire kayaks and canoes.

Wild *Escapes*

The Lazy Duck, Inverness-shire

Calling all lazy ducks – you can take it very easy indeed at this slow-living sanctuary among the soaring Scots pines of the Cairngorms National Park.

There are many ways to stay at The Lazy Duck, where a company of eco-friendly cabins, a safari tent and a tiny campsite (with space for just four tents) allow adventurers to hole up across this wild 2.4-ha (6-acre) landscape in any way they wish. The hidden gem here is The Woodman's Hut, a wooden cabin created using the living materials that surround it and with mammoth views of the mountains from the porch, where you can sit next to the crackling chimenea and be forgiven for thinking you've been transported to the Wild West. Inside, square windows cut into the log walls frame views of pines and snow-capped mountains. A Hebridean box bed (a wooden sleeping recess once commonly found in the cottages of the Highlands and the Hebrides) is tucked under a skylight, so you can stargaze your way to sleep each night.

> **The cabin is at its most magical in the calm of winter, when ice sits heavy on the boughs of the trees and you can stomp your way through snow to warm up by the wood burner**

You're an off-grid pioneer at The Lazy Duck, but the living in this cabin is still easy – lighting and a power bank mean you'll have juice once night falls, and there's a compost loo and rainwater shower. The cabin is at its most magical in the calm of winter, when ice sits heavy on the boughs of the trees and you can stomp your way through snow to warm up by the wood burner (there's unlimited firewood available to keep you toasty).

The second special stay here is at The Homestead, a meadow cabin that's all about the simple things. Friendly chickens roam outside the porch, and the communal fruit and veg patch is next door. If you don't fancy foraging for your own fare, you can also pick up a breakfast hamper of home-baked bread, homemade granola and freshly laid eggs from the farm's hens. The inside of the cabin is just one room, with comfy chairs, a kitchen corner and a hidden box bed. Outside, a hammock begs for an afternoon with a book under the whispering trees, perhaps with a dram of local Glenlivet whisky. And, of course, the ducks that give this place in the pines its name, bob on the nearby pond. If The Woodman's Hut is a winter warmer, The Homestead is what lazy summer days were made for.

The Duck's communal offerings are just as special – there's a wood-fired hot tub and a sauna available for guests to book, or you get your downward dog on with daily yoga sessions in the wood-clad wellbeing studio. Or venture further out-of-doors – moorland leads on to the Cairngorms National Park from here, where the forbidding Northern Corries and the Ryvoan Pass wind their way to the mountain town of Aviemore. The landscape around The Lazy Duck is one that shoves up close with the savage side of nature – 'this is a place for elemental living' promise the duck keepers, who run this haven in the Highlands.

Wild *Escapes*

On the doorstep

Hike to Ryvoan Bothy: This simple mountain bothy not far from Aviemore is a lovely place to shelter from inclement weather and have lunch mid-hike. From here you can also climb the steep flank of the hill behind it to reach Meall a' Bhuachaille's 810-m (2,657-ft) summit, making a 6-mile (3–4-hour) circular hike from the Glenmore Forest Park visitor centre.

Ski Scotland: When winter blankets the surrounding mountains in snow you can take to the Scottish slopes at the nearby Cairngorm Mountain Resort. A 30-minute drive from The Lazy Duck, the resort offers 18 miles of pistes to swish down, as well as guided Nordic cross-country skiing – a thrilling way to travel through the wilder corners of the National Park.

Opposite (top to bottom) Inside the Homestead cabin, which sits next to the owner's vegetable and flower garden. Spectacular views of the Cairngorm mountains.

Left: The cabin's kitchen and porch, where a log burner warms you late into the evening.

Right: Many cabins come with stripy hammocks to relax in.

Addresses and Websites

Abermydyr
Llanerchaeron, Ciliau Aeron, Aberaeron, Lampeter, SA48 8DG
www.nationaltrust.org.uk/holidays/wales/abermydyr

Bird How
Holmrook, Cumbria, CA19 1TH
www.nationaltrust.org.uk/holidays/lake-district/bird-how

Blacksmith's Cottage
Park Road, Blickling, Aylsham, Norwich, NR11 6NJ
www.nationaltrust.org.uk/holidays/norfolk/blacksmiths-cottage

The Boathouse at Knotts End
Oldchurch Bay, Penrith, Cumbria, CA11 0JJ
www.theboathouseatknottsend.com/

Boscastle Elm Cottage
New Mills, St Juliot, Boscastle, PL35 0BP
www.nationaltrust.org.uk/holidays/cornwall/boscastle-elm-cottage

The Boy John
Smugglers Cove, Frongoch Boatyard, Aberdyfi, Gwynedd,
Mid Wales, LL35 0RG
www.smugglerscove.info/boy_john.php

Brownsea Island
Brownsea Island, Poole, BH13 7EE
www.nationaltrust.org.uk/visit/dorset/brownsea-island

Bwthyn Mai
Beddgelert, Caernafon, LL55 4NG
www.nationaltrust.org.uk/holidays/wales/bwthyn-mai

Cartref
Hafod Y Llan, Nant Gwynant, Beddgelert, LL55 4NQ
www.nationaltrust.org.uk/holidays/wales/cartref

Chapel House Farm Campsite
Chapel House Farm, Craswall, Herefordshire, HR2 0PN
www.chapelhousefarm.com

Ditchling Cabin
Underhill Lane, Clayton, Hassocks BN6 8XE
www.ditchlingcabin.com/

Doyden Castle
Doyden, Port Quiin, Port Isaac, PL29 3SU
www.nationaltrust.org.uk/holidays/cornwall/doydon-castle

Dyffryn Mymbyr
Capel Curig, Betwsy Y Coed, Conwy, LL24 0ES
www.nationaltrust.org.uk/holidays/wales/dyffryn-mymbyr-farm-house

Eilean Shona
Acharacle, Argyll, PH36 4LR
www.eileanshona.com

Faraway Treehouse
Waingate Head, Kirklinton, Carlise, CA6 6BG
www.canopyandstars.co.uk/britain/england/cumbria/faraway-tree-house/faraway-treehouse

Farrs Meadow
Farrs Lodge, Cowgrove Road, BH21 4EL
www.farrsmeadow.co.uk/Farrs_Meadow/Home.html

Hafod Y Llan
Nant Gwynant, Caernarfon, Gwynedd, LL55 4NQ
www.nationaltrust.org.uk/holidays/wales/hafod-y-llan-campsite

The Lazy Duck
Nethy Bridge, Inverness-shire, PH25 3ED
www.lazyduck.co.uk

The Lazy T
Tylas Farm, York, YO62 5LH
www.thelazyt.co.uk/

Lickisto Blackhouse
1 Lickisto, Isle of Harris, HS3 3EL
www.lickistoblackhousecamping.co.uk

The Lodges at Longshaw Estate
Yarncliffe Lodge
Main Road, Nether Padley, Grindleford, Hope Valley, S32 2HE
www.nationaltrust.org.uk/holidays/peak-district-derbyshire/yarncliff-lodge
White Edge Lodge
Longshaw, Sheffield, S11 7TZ
www.nationaltrust.org.uk/holidays/peak-district-derbyshire/white-edge-lodge

Low Wray Campsite
Low Wray, Ambleside, Cumbria, LA22 0JA
www.nationaltrust.org.uk/holidays/lake-district/low-wray-campsite

Lyveden Cottage
Near Oundle, Northamptonshire, PE8 5AT
www.nationaltrust.org.uk/holidays/leicestershire-northamptonshire/
lyveden-cottage

North Lodge and River Cabin
Glen Dye Estate Office Bridge of Dye Steading, Strachan,
Banchory, AB31 6LT
www.glendyecabinsandcottages.com/north-lodge-and-cabin

Rhossili Old Rectory
Rhossili, West Gower, Swansea, SA3 1PL
www.nationaltrust.org.uk/holidays/wales/rhossili-old-rectory

Old Smock Mill
Benenden Road, Benenden, Cranbrook, TN17 4BU
www.oldsmockmill.com/

The Raft at Chigborough
Chigborough Farm, Chigborough Road, Maldon, CM9 4RE
www.canopyandstars.co.uk/britain/england/essex/chigborough-farm/
the-raft-at-chigborough

The Riverside
Broadmead Cut on River Wey, Ripley, Woking, GU23 7ES
www.canopyandstars.co.uk/britain/england/surrey/papercourt-lock/
the-riverside

Rockhouse Retreat
Honey Brook, Easthams Farm, Low Habberley, Worcestershire,
DY11 5RQ
www.therockhouseretreat.co.uk/

Rose Castle Cottage
Tarn Hows, Hawkshead Hill, LA22 8AQ
www.nationaltrust.org.uk/holidays/lake-district/rose-castle-cottage

The Round House
Ickworth Park, Bury St Edmunds, IP29 5RL
www.nationaltrust.org.uk/holidays/suffolk/round-house

Sally Port Cottage
St Mawes, Truro, TR2 5HA
www.ruralretreats.co.uk/england/cornwall-holiday-cottages/sal-
ly-port-cottage_cw045

Skoolie Stays
Little Thakeham Farm, Storrington Road, Thakeham,
Pulborough, R20 3EF
www.skooliestays.co.uk

Strand House
Cushendun, County Antrim, BT44 0PS
www.nationaltrust.org.uk/holidays/northern-ireland/strand-house

Tan Y Bwlch
Pwllheli, Gwynedd, LL53 8AD
www.nationaltrust.org.uk/holidays/wales/tan-y-bwlch

Trees
Beyond Fields, High Wray, Ambleside, LA22 0JQ
www.nationaltrust.org.uk/holidays/lake-district/trees

Troytown Campsite
Troytown Farm, St Agnes, Isles of Scilly, TR22 0PL
www.troytown.co.uk

Upper Booth Campsite
Edale, Hope Valley, Derbyshire, S33 7ZJ
www.nationaltrust.org.uk/holidays/peak-district-derbyshire/upper-
booth-farm-campsite

Warcleave Cottage
Chagford, Newton Abbot, TQ13 8JZ
www.nationaltrust.org.uk/holidays/devon/warcleave-cottage

Winnianton Farmhouse
Gunwalloe, Helston, TR12 7QE
www.nationaltrust.org.uk/holidays/cornwall/winnianton-farmhouse

Index